True Worship Experience

by
Reverend Eric Kwapong

True Worship Experience

Eric Kwapong

Pneuma Life Publishing
4451 Parliament Place
Lanham, MD 20706
www.pneumalife.com

CONTENTS

DEDICATION

To every Christian Leader and Believer who passionately desires a deeper walk and relationship with God's manifest presence through the True Worship Life.

To every Worship Minister, Song and Music Minister and Leader who desires to run with a new sense of mission and leadership maturity.

To all I have inspired and influenced positively in various ways into a deeper relationship with God.

To the coming generations who must and will carry on the torch of passion for God's presence through the True Worship Life 'til the Lord Jesus Christ comes back again - especially to our two beloved miracle children, Ayeyi and Inshira.

To my beloved Mother Mama and all my brothers and sisters Marian, Mercy, Joe, Mina, Emmanuel, and their spouses and children for their continuing love for God and their support for me.

To Rachel, the love of my life and true companion. You help me to fulfill my purpose and destiny.

ACKNOWLEDGMENTS

First, I am forever indebted to Almighty God to whom all true worship is due, for finding in me a vessel, molding me and making use of me to reveal His heart's desire to this generation.

I am always grateful to my precious wife and truest companion, Rachel, for your priceless support to my life and ministry. You always dare me to maximize my potential and fulfill my destiny. I love you. You began it all by urging me to write.

I thank God for the members and ministers of Praise Family Chapel International and partners and staff of His Presence Ministries whose faithfulness and prayers support me. I also appreciate those believers and well-wishers whose love, prayerful support and encouragement are always a great strength to me.

For the development and production of this book, I feel a deep sense of gratitude to: My beloved Mother "Mama" for always being there as pillar of support and for passionately praying til this book project was done.

Cephas Narh, a truly gifted and diligent editor, who pursued with me the development of this book from its early stages to its present form; and Mr. Derwin Stewart of Pneuma Life Publishing who believed in the material to publish this book.

Rev. John Ghartey, Ms. Josephine Medie, Dr. S. S. Quarcoopome and his wife Vanessa, Mrs. Mandy Hayford, Ms. Patricia Brown, Rev. Michael Essel and his wife Mrs. Evelyn Essel, Rev. Bernard Ankomah, Mr. Eric Odaame Beeko and Mrs. Theresa Beeko, Ms. Kedidia Mossi, and Ms. Saluwa Kazadi, for providing editorial services and moral encouragement to finish this work.

Dr. Myles Munroe, for your strong show of confidence, moral support and encouragement concerning this book project. Thank you for being the leader you are, and also putting me in contact with the publisher-Derwin Stewart.

Dr. Kingsley Fletcher and his wife, Pastor Martha Fletcher, for the encouragement and inspiration you have always given me. Thank you now and always.

I am eternally grateful to God for all my close circle of friends whose influence help to make me a better tool for God and a greater blessing to humankind.

Bishop T.D. Jakes, for your moral support and encouragement to me during the process of publishing this book. You are truly an inspiring example of a Leader. Thank you.

FOREWORD

There is nothing as natural to being human as worship. Innate within the human spirit is the deep desire to emulate and worship someone or something greater than self. From the dawn of time, in every culture, race, society and language, mankind has been a creature of worship. He is motivated by the desire to reach and pay homage to some power perceived to be greater than himself. Whether he worships the Supreme Being, God the Creator, the creature or the created thing, the soul of man reaches beyond himself to worship something.

The inherent love to worship is the spirit of relationship established by God that drives man to his Creator. When this desire for relationship is absent or misplaced, it results in destructive behavior that dilutes the purity and beauty of the human spirit.

Worship is defined as "to bow and pay homage, to kiss, to blow a kiss, or to be intimate with." In the context of the Christian church, worship takes the form of both individual and corporate. A multitude of expressions, methods, styles and contexts for worship exists. In many Christian churches, however, worship has become a mere form without substance.

Worship, in the context of the Bible, begins in the Garden of Eden where God walked and talked with Adam in the cool of the day. This casual, intimate, familiar relationship describes the kind of communion the Creator intended for mankind to have with Him. Since the Fall of man, that intimate relationship was broken. The spirit of man cries out for the restoration of this communion. The work of redemption through Jesus Christ provided the way for this relationship to be restored. Our Lord made provision for the Holy Spirit of God to return to the heart of man, thus reestablishing the communion between God and man.

The fallen spirit of man has to be retrained to appreciate this recovered communion, however. This is the reason behind the biblical command for individual and corporate worship. In the Old Testament, the system and pattern of worship involved a very complicated mandate. In the New Testament, from the ministry of Jesus, we learn that the new mandate for worship was to be transferred from form to spirit. The early church was birthed in the explosive fires of the baptism of the Holy Spirit, resulting in men saying, "We hear them speaking in our own tongues the wonderful works of God" (Acts 2:11).

Today there is a revival of the depth and gravity of this intimacy in worship. The waves of spiritual renewal worldwide over the past one hundred years have all been accompanied by a fresh expression of personal and corporate worship. Because of ignorance in this critical area, the worship experience has often been abused, misused, and lost. When this happens, we never fully enjoy the true purpose for the experience.

The Word of God states, "My people are destroyed for lack of knowledge" (Hos. 4:6). We must dedicate ourselves to study, learn, and understand this ultimate experience of personal relationship with God our Creator.

Eric Kwapong, in True Worship Experience, presents a fresh exposure of an age-old truth-worship. His historical and in-depth exploration of this subject provides the reader with the understanding, definitions, practical tools and spiritual insights that will make worship an exciting and fulfilling experience. His simple yet provocative approach to each aspect of this subject leaves one with a desire to worship. His articulate handling of many sensitive issues make this a book for all expressions of the body of Christ.

Rev. Kwapong will challenge your creativity and faith to express the true spirit of worship. His writing will establish a sense of purpose and motivate you to go beyond the familiar in worship. This book is a must for every believer who desires to refine his personal worship relationship, which in turn will result in a richer corporate worship experience.

I pray that every Christian leader will take the time to benefit from the investment, time, and experience of the author and enrich his or her own knowledge on this subject. After all, this is the reason why we come together as a corporate body. Read on, embrace the opportunity to enter the holy of holies, and let God walk and talk with you in the garden.

- Dr. Myles Munroe

PREFACE

Generations who seek only God's miracles and pro visions come and go, but they never serve and worship Him. Others are mainly interested in the personal gains of their Christian faith. My heart cry is that we will go beyond this "normal" Christian experience whose main focus and emphasis we have made the gains of our faith and begin taking seriously the primary responsibility of our most holy faith which is to worship him. My burning desire is that the body of Christ approaches this holy ministry of worship with a Scriptural understanding and a proper attitude. I want to see multitudes experience that tangible, manifested glory of Almighty God.

My burden is:

- That the manifested presence of God flows beyond the church's boundaries and touches the nations of the world, bringing total healing, restoration and revival.

- That the coming generations of leaders, both in this ministry and those overseeing the local church, will pursue a fuller development of this holy ministry of worship in the local church and around the world.

- That worship ministers develop mature leadership with a new sense of mission and purpose for this ministry.

- That the leadership of the local church will come to a greater understanding of this holy ministry and support it in every way possible.

- That the leadership of the local church-and these vessels in this ministry of music, praise and worship-will see themselves as partners on a common mission: to bring His Majesty's true worship and glory into the nations of the world.

The kingdoms of this world, which include its peoples, systems and philosophies, must become the kingdoms of our Christ and His Lord. The role of true worship in helping to accomplish all this will ultimately release the full glory of God into the nations of the world.

True worship is our primary entrance to the awesome glory of God's presence. My passion is for all of us to walk together through this gateway, because the full glory of the King must come in. Living in God's presence gives us a taste of heaven, which makes our tasks on earth a lot easier.

- Eric Kwapong

INTRODUCTION

The life of the church of Jesus Christ pivots on one very important truth, and that is worship and service to God. This is the first great truth every believer should be introduced to when he comes into the kingdom of God.

Today, all across the nations, every gathering of God's people is characterized by some kind of worship experience. This move, which is evident for all to see, is the restoration of true worship. Jesus talked about a time when true worshipers will worship the Father in spirit and in truth. The church today is at the threshold of a full experience of this prophecy. While some Christians show an appreciation of worship and engage in it with deeper meaning, worship to most Christians is a mere formality and meaningless ritual. The latter group is robbed of this most fulfilling experience because they lack a proper understanding of worship.

True worship expects to touch God. When this does not happen, the experience only makes the participants, at best, feel good about themselves, which, to say the least, is not enough. True worship denotes the general principle of giving, especially the giving of ourselves. All too often, however, we see the opposite. We normally exhibit a receiving mentality in worship. We are more used to receiving than giving, especially when we have to give with extra effort.

True worship is based on giving God our total love, which begins by offering our very lives. Even though our Christian walk begins with receiving Jesus as Lord and Savior, we first give ourselves to Him in response to what He did for us through His death and resurrection. On a daily basis we continue giving our love and commitment to God in every way. God wants His people to be more grounded in the attitude and spirit of giving. Worship, therefore, must be the church's lifestyle because God commands the church to render it to Him at all times.

The true worshiper is a giver in all respects-giving of his time and material substance in service to God, His people and His kingdom. It takes a great deal of effort to give God true worship out of love. Jesus said the true worshiper must worship God "in spirit and truth" (John 4:24). This means the true worshiper does not just "go through the motions" of worship, but he worships God with meaning.

The most obvious and common forms of worship as we express our love to God is through the beauty of singing and lifting up our hands. This holy ministry of worship is the believer's primary obligation to God. But Christians must be also rooted in the principle of giving as a lifestyle. Out of this, worship to God will be with understanding. We should acknowledge that worship and giving are very closely related. Giving has always been the foundation for true worship. It is therefore unbiblical and spiritually immature to worship God passively. Worship must be active, requiring conscious involvement.

Worship, like every other Christian experience, has a spirit dimension and a form. The spirit dimension must be expressed in form. In other words, the form conveys t he spirit. The spirit is discerned; the form is observed or seen. In the move of God in our day, the outward forms have gained such prominence over the spirit of worship that the forms have been reduced to what the Bible describes as the "letter," which kills. The apostle Paul contrasted the spirit and the letter, "The letter kills, but the Spirit gives life" (2 Cor. 3:6).

Obviously, therefore, worship that subsists only in forms without the spirit kills. It does not impart life; it does not touch the Object of our worship, who is God Almighty; it does not significantly bless the participants beyond giving them a "good feeling" of having been in the gathering of the saints.

One of the primary visible forms of worship is through music. This compounds the problem because many people can sing quite joyfully and do that very easily, too. Nevertheless, not everyone who sings is worshiping. Let's put it another way: Not every song containing lyrics from the Bible constitutes worship. Music permeates every gathering of the people of God, so it is easy to assume that because they are singing "cool" songs, the saints of God are engaged in worship. It is possible to go through these motions Sunday after Sunday and never touch God's heart.

As much as men can be sincere in their quest for something, if they miss the salient conditions necessary for the experience for which they yearn, they may not experience it at all-not because they had no intentions but because they lacked true knowledge and understanding. This is true of the worship experience. Because worship is so essential in the believer's walk with God, the saints must have a fuller understanding of what is involved so that they can have a meaningful worship experience and enrich their lives.

The Holy Spirit is ready to teach yearning and waiting hearts the "ins" and "outs" of worship so that the body of Christ can move into a much more relevant worship experience.

Anytime true worship takes place something significant happens. Why? Because worship touches the very heart of God. If we don't see significant things happening in our gatherings, then something must be wrong with our worship. It is our responsibility to ensure that we don't just go through the motions of worship. We must have real, meaningful worship in our services, such as "the Father is seeking" (John 4:23).

When this is done, the move of God becomes complete in us. We enjoy every part-both the tangible and intangible forms. As we discuss these issues with an open heart and a willingness to learn, greater illumination will come to us, and God will certainly lift us up from one degree of glory to another.

1

WHAT IS WORSHIP?

Worship is derived from an old English word worthship and denotes the worth of the individual receiving the special honors due to him in worship. Primarily, worship is that expression of our homage, which directly reflects our sense of value of our object of worship. It is especially used to express divine honors paid to a deity. Worship is therefore the honor, reverence and homage paid to any superior being or powers, whether men, angels or God. In our context, however, we refer to the worship of God Almighty.

Two personalities are involved in worship: the one giving and the One receiving. The receiver is God, our Father and Creator of the universe, who revealed Himself as the great I Am, who has given us salvation, who desires and deserves our worship. The giver is the believer who is God's child, created in His image. Your worship represents your evaluation of God, or how much you think He is worth.

Your worship is the key indicator of the value you put on Him.

Worship can further be defined as the quickening of the conscience by the holiness of God to live in abject submission to Him; to devote the will to God's purpose while also opening the heart to God's love.

The two most commonly used Hebrew and Greek expressions of the same word worship, are shachach and proskuneo, respectively, which appear 108 times in the Bible, suggest to "bow down in abject submission" or "prostrate" or do "obeisance" and "to kiss towards" (like a dog licks the master's hand). From these two words, true worship can be defined as a life of deep and abject submission, love, loyalty, dedication and absolute obedience to God. The striking thing here is that neither of these two words makes any direct reference to music, even though people have normally assumed that worship is simply singing and music. This is, indeed, a grave error.

The singing and music commonly associated with worship in the Christian church are only tools that we use to release to God a heart of submission, love, obedience, devotion and loyalty as our true worship. This means the singing and the music associated with worship should carry the spirit of true worship.

Let's further strengthen this argument by looking at this passage:

> These people draw near to Me with their mouth, and honor Me with their lips, but their heart is far from Me. And in vain they worship Me, teaching as

doctrines the commandments of men (Matt. 15:8-9).

The Lord Jesus Himself calls worship without the heart of true submission, obedience and love, vain worship. Vain worship is hypocritical, ritualistic and empty liturgy. It is meaningless and void of God's true presence. It is done because of tradition and on men's terms, not on God's terms. Jesus Christ Himself, who is the head of the church, rejects such worship.

> Now it came to pass after these things that God tested Abraham, and said to him, "Abraham!" and he said, "Here I am." And He said, "Take now your son, your only son Isaac, whom you love, and go to the land of Moriah, and offer him there as a burnt offering on one of the mountains of which I shall tell you." So Abraham rose early in the morning and . . . went to the place of which God had told him....And Abraham said to his young men, "Stay here with the donkey; the lad and I will go yonder and worship, and we will come back to you" (Gen. 22:1-3, 5).

Abraham had trusted God for almost twenty-five years to get this precious son in his old age. Then God said to him, "I want to test your love and obedience to Me." So He commanded Abraham, "Give back to Me this gift of a son, which represents twenty-five years of a hard won victory."

Abraham did not disobey. He "rose early in the morning and ...went to the place of which God had told him." According to Hebrews 11:17-19, "By faith Abraham, when he was tested, offered up Isaac, and he who had received the promises offered up his only begotten ...accounting that God was able to raise him up, even from the dead."

Abraham rose early, went by faith and offered up Isaac, counting his son already dead in his heart because he knew God meant business with him. As we know from the Genesis account, Abraham did not finally "kill" his son. The Book of Hebrews says he "offered up Isaac," meaning true obedience and submission had already taken place in his heart. As far as he was concerned, Isaac, his only son, was already sacrificed. He demonstrated true obedience, submission and the triumph of love for God. Abraham called it worship.

Based on this example, true worship is obedience, love and abject submission. It's not just singing, playing music or having church. True worship is displayed to the point of death to self and where the Lord Jesus Christ reigns ultimately in our lives.

> I beseech you therefore, brethren, by the mercies of God, that you present your bodies a living sacrifice, holy, acceptable to God, which is your reasonable service (Rom. 12:1).

Notice the strong assertion by the apostle Paul that when our lives become a living sacrifice, holy and acceptable to God on His terms and not on ours, this becomes our reasonable service. Or, as the New International Version puts it, your "spiritual act of worship."

> And behold, a woman in the city who was a sinner, when she knew that Jesus sat at the table in the Pharisee's house, brought an alabaster flask of fragrant oil, and stood at His feet behind Him weeping; and she began to wash His feet with her tears, and wiped them with the hair of her head; and she

kissed His feet and anointed them with the fragrant
oil.... [Jesus said to Simon], "You gave Me no
kiss, but this woman has not ceased to kiss
My feet since the time I came in.... Her sins,
which are many, are forgiven, for she loved
much . . ." (Luke 7:37-38, 45, 47).

As the Holy Spirit opened my eyes, I saw the totality
of true worship ministered by this woman to the Lord Jesus
Christ.

Note these points:

- She was a sinner who brought Jesus a flask of fragrant oil-meaning she came with her material treasure, which she got out of her sweat and toil, her
  first expression of worship.

- She stood at Jesus' feet weeping-meaning she came
  to the feet where sins are forgiven, in a true spirit
  of brokenness, submission and gratitude for what
  Jesus now meant to her. A truly broken, humble,
  submitted and grateful attitude was her expression
  of worship.

- She began to wash His feet with her tears-mean-
  ing she poured out tears of gratitude at the feet
  where real work and kingdom business is done.
  The feet move the rest of the body forward. The
  parallel is that real kingdom work is what moves
  God's kingdom forward. Her worship progressed
  to work and a labor of love for the kingdom of
  God and for Christ's sake.

A few times in the Bible, worship is translated as work (from the Hebrew), obviously being the work of God's kingdom.

- She wiped Jesus' feet with her hair. A woman's hair is her pride and glory (1 Cor. 11:15). She invested into the kingdom work of God all her glory-influence, power, substance, etc. The high expression of her worship was to give the very basis of her dignity, and all she had toiled for-her glory-to the Master.

- She kissed His feet and anointed them. She was ready to totally dispense of her treasure, now ready to let the fragrance of her worship be poured into Jesus' life to move the cause of God's kingdom forward. She kissed His feet, which in our context is symbolic of true worship. (Remember worship in the New Testament is to "kiss towards.") Her worship climaxed with lavishing love on the Master, endlessly kissing the feet. If she could come this far in worship, then no wonder she could break the treasure box and anoint the Master's feet.

Note: At the point of true worship, the physical evidence is almost always an absolute readiness to dispense of one's self, energy and material substance for the true cause of Christ.

Referring to her acts, Jesus said she "loved much." Remember that the foundation of true worship is loving the Lord. This passage suggests that true worship begins with a genuine readiness to dispense of one's material treasure in the spirit of true brokenness and gratitude, a burning desire to promote the cause of Christ and absolute love for God.

The worship of God, therefore, involves an acknowledgment of God's divine perfection and a submission to His nature. Worship presupposes that men can know God, and that His perfection sets Him far above men.

True worship is also the intense and grateful response to God when the heart is filled with the deep sense of appreciation for the blessings bestowed upon us from on high. Honor and adoration are rendered to God by reason of what He is in Himself and what He is to those who render it.

We can also say that liturgy, which is the entirety of the scheduled worship services of the corporate gatherings of the Christian church, is also worship. It is for this reason that the personal life of the individual Christian should constitute a life of daily worship, in and out of these corporate gatherings. Remember that always and primarily, our gathering as God's people "is unto Him."

God Sees More Than Fruit

Let me illustrate the concept of worship using the example of a tree. A tree has a base, which is often the roots but also includes the soil, then the stem, branches and leaves, which eventually bear the fruit.

Most people are more interested in the fruit than in any other part of the tree. We focus on the fruit and almost always neglect the other parts. The roots, stem, branches, leaves and fruit have a holistic existence and are not separate from each other. Without one, the others are incomplete.

7

In its final form worship can also be seen as having a base, a stem, branches and, eventually, fruit. The base gives rise to the stem before the fruit shows. The fruit therefore is not separate or divorced from the rest of the tree (stem and base).

In the same way, according to Hebrews 13:15, we are to present some of the expressions of our worship as the "fruit of our lips," but the presupposition is that the fruit should be a natural and integral part of the stem and base of a full "tree" of worship.

This is to say that the fruit alone, which is singing, lifting the hands, bowing, kneeling, playing instruments and all the other visible expressions do not in themselves constitute true worship.

Let us discuss these other lost parts in the totality of worship.

The Base

The base (roots and soil) in our context represents a truly yielded heart (root) submitted to God (soil).

A heart that is completely yielded to God must be at the base of any worship experience. We know that the foolish heart cannot worship God because it says there is no God (Ps. 14:1). Neither can a carnal, unspiritual heart truly worship (1 Cor. 2:14). Let's remember that Jesus said, "The true worshipers will worship the Father in spirit and truth" (John 4:23). False worship, as opposed to what the Bible calls "worship in truth," does not have a truly yielded heart as its base.

A heart that does not recognize the highest authority, which is God, makes it impossible for any true worship to take place.

The Stem

The stem is a passage for all the nutrients to travel from the soil to the upper part of the plant. Think of the stem in terms of linkage.

The stem joins the lower and upper parts of a tree. The stem, therefore, can be seen as the vital connection between the base and its fruit. This analogy explains our relationship with God as the "vital connection" between our truly yielded heart and fruit of worship, which is a very important component in the worship experience. For example: the only reason a child looks up to its mother is because a relationship exists between them. What makes mother different from any other woman? Mother immediately suggests a relationship.

In John 4:23 Jesus says, "True worshipers will worship the Father." Whenever we talk of God as our Father, we establish our special relationship to Him as a Creator. A truly healthy, unbroken relationship with God is the other natural and integral component of the true worship experience.

The apostle Paul visited Athens and saw an altar with this inscription, "To the unknown God" (Acts 17:23). Paul explained that the God they sought to worship could be known. He obviously wondered, "How can you worship a God with whom you do not have a relationship?"

Therefore, true worship becomes a flow beginning with a heart truly submitted to God, resulting in a healthy relationship with Him and culminating in the visible "fruits" of worship.

The Fruits

As stated earlier, God enjoys our worship as a holistic entity and responds with the release of His presence. If the base and stem of the tree are bad, then the fruit will also be bad. If the base and stem of our worship lives are bad, then our fruit of worship will also be bad. God will not enjoy our worship as a "sweet smelling savor." If the fruit of worship has no base-a heart yielded to God-and no stem-an active, dynamic and healthy relationship with God-then true worship has not taken place.

When we see people singing with upraised hands, we conclude they are engaged in worship. Or when we see people kneel or fall flat with their faces on the floor, we conclude that they must be worshiping. What we visibly "see" is not all that worship constitutes. This is why I have used the analogy of the tree to explain true worship. God sees the whole tree of our lives, not just the fruit of our lips. Our base and stem need to be just as acceptable to God.

Fruit is a natural part of a tree, and worship should come naturally for the believer. True worship flows from a base-a truly submitted heart of obedience-and is girded by the stem-an active relationship with God-which results in the "fruit," the visible expressions of worship.

Can you understand why believers are referred to as "trees of righteousness"? (Isa. 61:3). This is because your total being is the "tree of His worship" and also the temple of His worship. You are God's instrument of true worship.

Worship, therefore, is the phenomenon in which men, out of a heart of absolute submission, render appreciation to God through the context of a dynamic and healthy relationship existing between man (the worshiper) and God (our object of worship).

2

THE ORIGIN OF WORSHIP

Worship begins with a God who is all-powerful, all-knowing and ever-present. Worship originates from an intense desire both within God and man for fellowship. In human terms, this desire can best be described as a void that must be filled. When something needs to be filled, you must pour into it. God is drawn toward fellowship, not with Himself, but with other beings made in His image-that is, you and me.

It is difficult to describe this phenomenon in human language without the risk of committing any theological errors. We cannot think of the all-powerful, self-sufficient God as having lack within Himself, but there appears to be what could be thought of as an "absence" within God Himself, which can only be filled through a kind of fellowship. To appreciate this intense desire in Almighty God, let us explore this scenario presented by the writer of Proverbs.

> There are three things which are too wonderful for me, yes, four which I do not understand: The way of an eagle in the air, the way of a serpent on a rock, the way of a ship in the midst of the sea, and the way of a man with a virgin (Prov. 30:18-19).

Let us explore this mystery: "the way of a man with a virgin." The first manifestation of this can be traced to the Garden of Eden when Adam exclaimed, "This is now bone of my bones and flesh of my flesh" (Gen. 2:23). The excitement, the joy, the fulfillment that ran through Adam's entire being as he embraced his bride cannot be easily ascertained on the written page. That must have been a wonderful experience for both Adam and Eve. In the same way, for you to understand this, you may have to experience what Adam experienced.

Let me attempt to explain Adam's statement to Eve. Adam was admiring that which "came out of him." Eve was in Adam before she was taken out of him. In effect, Adam saw the part of him that went out. It was like a "lost and found" situation. Adam was saying, "How exciting to have you back!" This, which the writer describes as the way of a man with a virgin, is an eternal manifestation of the phenomenon of one person finding the "lost" part of his being.

Normally a man's heart does not beat when he sees another man as it does when he sees a woman-the part that was taken out of him and formed into another like being. Are the pieces coming together now?

This is my argument: Man came out of God!

The dust of the earth didn't make man. It was the breath of God that came out of Him that made Adam. This intense desire of God for fellowship with a part of Him that is "out there" gave birth to and sustains the mystery of worship. Whenever God looks at man, He sees a part of Himself and gets drawn to him.

When the psalmist said, "O Lord, our Lord, how excellent is Your Name in all the earth" (Ps. 8:1), it boggled his imagination that this great God should seek the fellowship of a mere man, and so he asks, "When I consider Your heavens, the work of Your fingers, the moon and the stars, which You have ordained, what is man that You are mindful of him, and the son of man that You visit him?" (vv. 3-4). In the psalmist's mind, God should be satisfied with the beauty of the universe that speaks volumes about His greatness. Nevertheless, God looks beyond all that to give special attention to man. The truth is that none of those beautiful things is as much a part of God. None bears His image and likeness as man does. God's "hunger" for the fellowship of worship goes to His "image and likeness" out there-man! This is what makes the difference!

A close study of God's redemption plan from the Fall of man through Jesus' death and resurrection, up to the present time unfolds the mystery of God's desire for man's fellowship. The fact that God took the first step to reconcile and restore the broken relationship with man, for the ultimate purpose of fellowship, is a testimony of His "hunger" for man.

Come to think of it, the price He had to pay (the precious blood of Jesus) is awesome-all for this love of fellowship again. Why did He do it? Out of this fellowship God receives quality worship-that which is done out of choice, motivated and sustained through an individual and personal relationship with God.

Man's response to the "hunger" of God for him is quality worship.

God's relationship with Israel is similar to a man in love with a wayward woman. Even with the very harsh statements God made to Israel, one could always discern a beckoning to Israel to come back to Him. We, therefore, have to understand that in God's relationship with man, the only aspect that goes to God is worship. Man takes all the benefits of this relationship-healing, deliverance, divine provision and several others.

If God would do everything-including the sacrifice of His only Son-to have the relationship restored, you can understand the intensity of God's pleasure in worship and the fulfillment He gets when His subjects worship Him. This means the ultimate purpose even for salvation is for God to derive the utmost pleasure of worship. The ultimate of salvation in Jesus is not healing, deliverance, protection, prosperity, etc. It is God's "invitation package" to us to come into a fellowship of love where He gets our worship.

> Thou art worthy, O Lord, to receive glory and honour and power: for thou hast created all things, and for thy pleasure they are and were created (Rev. 4:11, KJV).

This verse substantiates the fact that the obvious, ultimate reason for creation is for God to derive utmost pleasure, which is worship.

Worship, however, did not start with the creation of man. The Bible records that before God created man in His image, He lived in heaven with the angels worshiping Him. The apostle John caught a glimpse of the Almighty sitting on His throne and brought this report to mankind.

> After these things I looked, and behold, a door standing opened in heaven. And the first voice which I heard was like a trumpet speaking with me.... Immediately I was in the Spirit; and behold, a throne set in heaven, and One sat on the throne.... The twenty-four elders fall down before Him who sits on the throne and worship Him who lives forever and ever, and cast their crowns before the throne, saying: "You are worthy, O Lord, to receive glory and honor and power; for You created all things, and by Your will they exist and were created" (Rev. 4:1-2, 10-11).

It is evident from John's report that he was not just seeing something that took place in the past or something that occurred only at that time or what would take place in the future. He saw the past, present and future all at once. Since it is not easy to establish how far into the past he saw and how far into the future, we are right to conclude that what he saw happens eternally. Now that introduces a very important truth to explore. God must have established what John saw, and the reason for establishing something that occurs with no time limit on it is simple: God loves worship! He cherishes it! He wants it! It is the ultimate reason He poured out of Himself the creative power to make all of creation, so that everything would come back to Him in worship.

A "Hunger" for Fellowship

Let us explore another analogy. Consider the joy of a mother when she gives birth to a child. All her family and friends rejoice with her. Everyone sees her joy as a result of the newborn, especially when one thinks of the nine months of pregnancy followed by the labor pains. What everyone forgets is that the joy of holding the baby in her arms existed long before that baby was conceived. From the beginning, this joyful mother had within her the potential and ability to give birth to another human being who would be a "part of her." The point is one can't help but be in love and joyful fellowship with another person who is a part of him or her.

Normally most women express a deep desire to have their own child. A woman narrates how she would take care of the child, and-especially if it is a girl- how she would dress her and fix her hair. The story does not end here. Before she even gets pregnant within a legitimate marriage, she has in mind the kind of relationship she wants to have with her child. In essence, before any child is born, the hunger for fellowship between mother and child already exists. When it comes to this relationship, she expects the child to look to her as mother; as the earthly source of sustenance, refuge and protector; as one on whom the child's earthly existence depends. Now all these exist long before the mother ever thinks of having a baby. It is in pursuing the fulfillment of this "hunger" that the mother conceives and bears a child. Thus, the child becomes the source of joy and the reason for fellowship.

Now you can understand one of God's prime motivations in creating man, especially the reason He created man in His image. God must have been motivated by the possibility of having worship from a subject better than the angels. He looked for a subject whose worship would come by an act of the will-one who had the choice to love and worship Him. Man's creation was therefore the result of the "hunger" in God for worship, as in the case of the mother's "hunger" for fellowship with her child.

Before man was created, the angels offered to God His pleasure-His will and His joy-because it was an express obligation for them. They did not do it by choice. Let's examine Ezekiel 28:12-19.

Here we find that Lucifer was created as the embodiment of music. God fashioned him that way so he could lead the angels in worship to God. This establishes the truth that God loves worship. When Lucifer fell, however, a big gap was created. God had made a key investment that was lost in Lucifer's rebellion.

God decided that the subject of worship must now do it not by obligation, but by choice. If you do something by choice, you do it willingly-not by force. It comes from your heart and that, obviously, must be of a higher quality.

God expects worship from all creation with understanding and on this basis: true worship is out of one's own initiative and free will to love God. This becomes a choice one makes to worship Him. The category of subjects expected to give worship to God can be seen in these verses:

> All nations whom you have made shall come and worship before You, O Lord, and shall glorify Your name (Ps. 86:9).

> All the ends of the world shall remember and turn to the Lord, and all the families the nations shall worship before You (Ps. 22:27).

> Praise Him, all His angels; praise Him, all His hosts (Ps. 148:2).

The hosts of the Lord include all inanimate creation, plant and animal life, angels and all humankind. The church of Jesus Christ is also considered corporately as a host of the Lord. The word host means company, group or category.

Writing under the inspiration of the Holy Spirit, King David makes us understand what has always been there-God's desire that all His creation should worship Him. This pleasure and intense desire existed before all things were created. Great and small, rich and poor, tall and short, all colors, races, genders and people of every social status were made to fulfill this desire of God.

Let us look at the event described as the "triumphant entry into Jerusalem" as recorded in Luke 19:37-38.

> [As Jesus drew near] the descent of the Mount of Olives, the whole multitude of the disciples began to rejoice and praise God with a loud voice for all the mighty works they had seen, saying, "Blessed is the King who comes in the name of the Lord! Peace in heaven and glory in the highest!"

Some of the Pharisees immediately reacted, wanting Jesus to rebuke them. Notice Jesus' answer:

"I tell you that if these should keep silent, the stones would immediately cry out" (Luke 19:40).

Jesus' answer should settle every doubt in our minds concerning the importance God attaches to worship. Worship is so important to God that if the highest category of His creation refuses to worship Him, He will turn to His other creations for worship. This is a serious thing if it should ever happen! Indeed this is terrible that God would turn to His inanimate creation for worship because the "rightful and legitimate worshipers" refuse to do it.

Worship originates from this deep hunger inside man for God, and also the hunger inside God to be restored to His creation in a love relationship. The angels do not have it; animals and vegetation do not have it.

We can conclude that even though God expects worship from all creation, worship from man means a lot more to God than any of His creatures. Only man was created to offer worship in a direct relationship with God. He is to render it with the power of his choice and free will.

3

THE SPIRIT OF WORSHIP

Although the discourse with the woman at the well in John 4 eventually led to the salvation of many in the city of Samaria, Jesus also used the opportunity to teach a very profound truth about worship. Jesus said to her:

> Woman, believe Me, the hour is coming when you will neither on this mountain, nor in Jerusalem, worship the Father. You worship what you do not know; we know what we worship, for salvation is of the Jews. But the hour is coming, and now is, when the true worshipers will worship the Father in spirit and truth; for the Father is seeking such to worship Him. God is Spirit, and those who worship Him must worship in spirit and truth (John 4:21-24).

This passage represents the most profound, revolutionary truths Jesus ever taught about worship. Jesus spoke of a drastic change in the understanding, pattern, attitudes and totality of worship. Consider this question: "What is it in worship that blesses God and makes a response from Him inevitable, a matter of course and, to put it more bluntly, an obligation?"

What does God see in a people who have gathered with their hands lifted up, or in whatever posture their bodies may be, that prompts Him to instantly "come down" and strongly manifest Himself in their gathering?

The answer: A spirit of worship-not just the visible expressions of worship. The worship of God takes place in the deepest place of our entire beings, deeper than our thoughts, feelings and will. It takes place in our spirits.

Worship is man's spirit activated or stirred up to relate to God in a creature-Creator relationship in its absolute terms. For the child of God, this takes place within the context of a son-Father relationship.

In whatever terms we define the relationship, the spirit of worship is the human spirit in a realm where what matters is the awesomeness of God and nothing more. All other issues are relegated to second place. This truth, however, is not often experienced during the corporate worship service. For many, this has been substituted with emotions, ecstasy, frenzy or a "charged" atmosphere. To others, having a serious and pious demeanor while being "cool" means they are "in the spirit."

To worship God in spirit means there is a spirit of worship present in our worship lives that is expressed in various visible forms. The other aspect of worship expressed in form is "worship in truth." Truth, according to John 17:17, is God's Word. This same word brings form, direction, shape and "flesh" to that which is activated from within. The worship forms with which we are familiar are actually containers.

The spirit of worship is the real substance of worship. This spirit is released as a result of a heart in deep and total submission to God. It does not come from God; it originates from man to God as a "sweet smelling sacrifice."

One cannot touch the spirit of worship, neither can one define it. It may have other "colors" that attempt to describe it, but these do it rather imperfectly. As soon as God encounters that "spirit," the whole worship service changes. His presence fills the gathering, which is now characterized by tangible manifestations of God's glory.

The spirit of worship also stems from a deep relationship with and knowing of God. This knowing is not mental. It does not just reside in our imaginations. We cannot just imagine God and worship Him that deeply. We must know Him in a healthy, dynamic relationship. That knowing does not only belong to the realm of the soul. The soul only feels and imagines it and tries to understand, but your "inside man" captures the real experience of who God is, especially in relation to yourself.

I recall my own frustrations and utter disappointment about two decades ago when I was in a typical Pentecostal/charismatic service. I was trying to be "in the spirit" by imitating whatever I saw others doing in the service. Some were screaming and crying while others were praying with a lot of tears. At one point the minister leading the service made things even worse for me by giving the congregation some confusing instructions. He said, "Everybody drink ye the blood in the Holy Ghost!" Oh my goodness! In my growing desperation (at that point my eyes were closed), I opened my eyes to see if there was any "blood" flowing. I wanted by all means to "feel" something dramatic going down my spine because I thought that was "life in the spirit" and "worship in spirit." The good news is, in growing up as a Christian and a minister over the years, I began to properly understand and appreciate that "life in the spirit" or "worship in spirit" does not subsist on emotions, ecstasy, frenzy or even tears. It begins first with a truly dynamic relationship with God through living under and submitting to the Lordship and authority of Jesus on a daily basis. This is the foundation of worship in spirit.

To worship God "in spirit" therefore simply begins with a relationship and association with Him. Our reference passage declares, "The true worshipers will worship the Father in spirit and truth." The spirit of worship therefore is released from our personal knowing and walking with Him as our Father. Jesus taught us in our praying to acknowledge God as "our Father."

The nation of Israel did not know Him as Father. They knew Him as the God of their fathers-Abraham, Isaac, and Jacob. Abraham himself came as close as "friend," but because of Jesus we know God now as our Father. The knowledge and practical experience of this truth releases within us the spirit of worship, and then we can truly "worship in spirit."

God's Presence Consciousness

To worship "in spirit" or, better still, the spirit of worship, means to worship with a consciousness of God's presence. By faith, we know that:

> As God has said, "I will dwell in them and walk among them. I will be their God, and they shall be My people.... I will be a Father to you, and you shall be My sons and daughters, says the Lord Almighty" (2 Cor. 6:16, 18).

The spirit of worship produces a consciousness of the reality of the existence of God. Such consciousness also carries with it a knowing of who God is. As this consciousness grows, the individual gradually becomes oblivious to the presence of everyone surrounding him. The eyes may be open or, better still, closed. The ears nevertheless may be wide open and hearing the rich music in the corporate worship environment, but none of these has enough power to interrupt the individual's focus on the knowledge that God is around them wherever they may be.

God is not a nonresident Father; neither are we absentee children. He said He will dwell, walk, live and abide with us. This means we who are His children, washed in the blood of Jesus, will live daily in His presence. He said, "I will never leave you nor forsake you" (Heb. 13:5). We are in His presence daily though we may not "feel it" or are even aware of it.

As we learn to practice living in a greater consciousness of His presence and fellowship with Him, whether in the privacy of our daily lives or in the corporate service, the spirit of worship is released, and we will be worshiping in spirit. Certainly there will be greater dimensions and depths of this phenomena, but no depth is too much for us to enjoy and dare to explore.

"Tug and Pull"

In chapter two, I explained what happens between mother and child and how that speaks about the origin of worship. The bond between mother and child (arising from the unique relationship) is parallel to the "spirit of worship" released from the true worshiper toward his heavenly Father. Something inside the child "tugs" and "pulls" him toward his mother and recognizes her person and presence. It's the same situation between the true worshiper and God who is Spirit.

> For this is the covenant that I will make with the house of Israel after those days, says the Lord: I will put My laws in their mind and write them on their hearts; and I will be their God, and they shall be My people. None of them shall teach his neighbor, and none his brother, saying, "Know the Lord," for all shall know Me, from the least of them to the greatest of them (Heb. 8:10-11).

Notice these various phrases: "I will put My laws in their (your) mind and write them on their (your) hearts; and I will be their (your) God, and they (you) shall be My people." These powerful phrases lay the foundation for the kind of relationship God now has with the New Testament worshiper, which is different from His relationship with the Old Testament worshiper. The latter related to the God of their father, Abraham, on tablets of stones from the "outside." The New Testament worshiper has the laws of God on his mind and heart, which means "something on the inside" will naturally be released to express worship. The spirit of worship will be there on the inside when people come to know the Father through Jesus Christ.

There will be the natural "tug" and "pull" to worship God the Father as is the case between mother and child. This is a supernatural work of the Holy Spirit within the worshiper from the onset of the new birth. Notice the phrase in the passage: "None of them shall teach his neighbor...saying, 'Know [worship] the Lord,' for all shall know [worship] Me, from the least of them to the greatest." This is why the New Testament believer is a worshiper who carries inside him the "spirit of true worship," without necessarily being taught and instructed.

For instance, who told that growing toddler, "This is your mom coming"? It is the bond that has been there from the womb.

Even though the spirit of worship is always ready to be released in the atmosphere of true worship, the spirit of worship is always present in the heart of the worshiper. In any corporate service, until the spirit of worship grips the hearts of men, no true worship can take place. Like the child, the believer who learns to live daily in God's presence expresses his love to God in various forms without necessarily being "instructed" to do so.

The spirit of worship is released in our walk with God, as we learn to live daily in the Lord's presence "from the least of them to the greatest," the most inexperienced believer to the most experienced believer.

We can take another example of the relationship between a loving, happily married couple. When the marriage relationship is being kept, nourished and nurtured, the "spirit of love" grows. Others experience the opposite. The "spirit of hatred" takes over because the relationship is broken and destroyed. When our relationship with God is destroyed with sin, the spirit of worship dies and the true worship experience becomes an illusion.

Faith

The spirit of worship produces expectancy, or faith, in the believer. The primary characteristic of this faith is that God will respond to the believer as he remains in His presence, fully consumed by the knowledge of God and totally submitted to Him in thought, emotion and will.

This expression of faith is powerful, irresistible to God, and leaves Him with only one option-to respond. The response man should expect from God is not for Him to do anything tangible in particular for him. It should be the response for fellowship, a confirmation of the Father-son relationship God has with all who have believed Jesus Christ as their personal Savior. When this happens, God will normally always meet our other physical, emotional, material and spiritual needs because He knows that our primary motive for worship is to love Him and not so much having our needs met.

At this point we also communicate with God, not through the mind but by our human spirits. Communication takes place between similar natures. That's why the mind, or emotion alone, cannot worship God enough. The greatness of God is revealed not to the mind but first to the human spirit. It is the revelation of God to the believer that produces reverence in the believer.

Faith also produces reverence, which culminates in the complete submission of man's ego, his human self, his thoughts, his emotions and even his will to the greatness of God.

Meditation

There is a mental posture in worship, and when worship overwhelms, the spirit of worship also culminates in meditation. Meditation suggests a kind of positive wrestling with God. Meditation involves feeding so richly on God's Word until you can muse (speak to yourself) in the Word. It is being consumed so totally with God, His attributes and nature until your mind is captured with the awesomeness of His goodness you have personally enjoyed.

When we bask in the spirit of worship, at its peak we are captured and lost in the awe of God's greatness, His holiness and attributes. His nature and attributes of mercy and love consume us. Meditation on who God is and the revelation of the things He has created for man to enjoy is therefore one prime characteristic of the spirit of worship. Such meditation produces nothing short of a verbalization that touches the very heart of God and prompts His desire for fellowship with man.

Let's consider the words of the song: "If it had not been for the Lord on my side, tell me where would I be?" (Composed from Psalm 124:1-8.)

31

This verbalization is a direct product of the second kind of meditation. It takes the individual through a panorama of the events of his life, from birth to the present moment. Out of a mixture of both pleasant and unpleasant experiences, the individual appears to be left with one conclusion: God must be the only reason why the individual continues to be alive. If the individual happens to have experienced the new birth, then his heart becomes lightened since that is the greatest miracle that could happen to him.

Meditation involves the total being of man. The human spirit focuses on God, drawing the mind's attention to the interventions of God in the natural affairs of the individual. The mind recalls the events as best as possible. The mind needs the human spirit, and the spirit needs the human mind in meditation. The mind functions as a memory organ and collates issues from the natural world. Nevertheless the mind alone is not able to properly interpret the events of life in the context of God's love and His purposes for mankind.

There can be no experience of the spirit of worship without meditation. It is through meditation that the entire being of man is saturated with the desire and the joy of wanting to abide continually in the presence of God.

The meditations produced by the spirit of worship have the power of transforming our every circumstance into praise and thanksgiving to God.

Characteristics of True Worship

In understanding the attitudes that characterize the spirit of worship, let us explore the story of the woman who came with the alabaster box of ointment and poured its contents on Jesus' feet.

> And behold, a woman in the city who was a sinner, when she knew that Jesus sat at the table in the Pharisee's house, brought an alabaster flask of fragrant oil, and stood at His feet behind Him weeping; and she began to wash His feet with her tears, and wiped them with the hair of her head; and she kissed His feet and anointed them with the fragrant oil (Luke 7:37-38).

Brokenness

By her tears, the woman portrayed brokenness of spirit. King David understood the value of brokenness before God, which led him to say, "The sacrifices of God are a broken spirit, a broken and contrite heart-these, O God, You will not despise" (Ps. 51:17).

"Broken" in the Hebrew is dakah, which means "to crumble, to beat into pieces, to bruise, crush, or to humble." It is characteristic of one yielded to the Lordship of our master Jesus Christ. God does not do this "breaking" of the spirit and of self. It is a result of the human spirit filled with the sovereignty, authority, Lordship and awesomeness of God such that the person loses his "essence" as an individual. Such a loss of individuality is permitted only before God. If it happens before man, it is dangerous and could even incur God's displeasure. It tells God, "I am humble and broken before You, and You are the only One who can put me together again." It means if God does not exalt the individual, he is of no value.

33

If you think of the woman's background, you understand that she was truly broken. She was described as a sinner. She admitted before Jesus that she had no value except the value He placed on her. This brokenness tells God, "Every greatness I have is because of You, and I worship You with everything I am and have!"

How can God see brokenness in a man's spirit and gloss over it? That will never happen! Knowledge of this truth inspired the psalmist to say, "A broken and contrite heart-these, O God, You will not despise" (Ps. 51:17).

Humility

When the woman used her hair to wipe Jesus' feet, that act underscored her lowliness and humility. Scripture tells us that the glory of the woman is her hair. She made herself of no reputation. She bowed before Jesus. This is characteristic of the spirit of true worship. It produces within us a humble, burning passion to pour our lives into the service of our Lord Jesus Christ.

Love

Jesus Himself testified to the love the woman expressed toward her Savior and Redeemer, her Lord and King, when He said, "Therefore I say to you, her sins, which are many, are forgiven, for she loved much. But to whom little is forgiven, the same loves little" (Luke 7:47).

She poured out love in an unashamed, nonsexual manner. This she demonstrated in kissing Jesus' feet. Worship devoid of love is but an empty, outward show of hypocrisy.

Remember that the most commonly used word for worship in the New Testament is proskuneo, which is to kiss. Kissing is a truly legitimate and morally sound expression of the dearest love. Kissing Jesus' feet poured out a most profound love in abject submission, which characterizes the true spirit of worship.

Giving

Bible scholars estimate the alabaster box of ointment as a very costly family treasure. Regardless of the cost, she was ready to give it to her Savior and Lord. She did not give it as surplus but as her very best. She demonstrated King David's vow not to give anything that has no value. He said, "Nor will I offer burnt offerings to the LORD my God with that which costs me nothing" (2 Sam. 24:24). That means in all our worship the most valuable things must be presented.

Our worship is not complete without quality giving. True worship is not only the giving of ourselves, but it is also the giving of our material substance. The physical act of giving is a key manifestation of the willingness in the heart to give, which is also a true characteristic of the spirit of worship.

Conclusion

All of these attributes, including the depth of understanding with which people worship, indicate the spirit of worship. The consummation of the spirit of worship releases the mouth to speak and the body to move in a certain way, or the individual to worship in a certain manner. Without the spirit of true worship, our worship is like any other religion or cultic practice expressed in empty forms.

4

WORSHIP FORMS

The potential for worship resides within you. The preceding chapters explained the spirit of worship. If it stands by itself, the spirit of worship cannot be fully understood by the observer. For example, how do we know that someone is humble before God? How can we tell if a person understands the greatness of God? What does a submissive spirit look like? These questions are very difficult for us to answer.

Every experience we go through must find expression in the physical because that is how we have been made. We have a physical body, and we live on a physical earth on which a lot of physical activity takes place. So it must be with our highest ministry to God on earth-worship. There has to be visible expression because God takes pleasure in the physical expression of worship locked inside us. God commands us to worship not only in spirit but also in truth

(John 4:24). The truth of God's Word brings direction, form and physical expression to our worship.

The spirit of worship must not remain locked in the heart but must be released through your body. When we say forms of worship, we simply mean expressing our worship physically and visibly. Even though the Bible says that God looks on the heart, for our own sakes Jesus wants worship to be expressed physically because that expression must be real and alive even to us.

You will have faith in the expression of worship that you give to God as a sacrifice of gratitude and thanksgiving coming from your own heart. Hebrew 13:15 refers to those expressions of worship as "fruit."

One of the great leaders of the Bible shared his life of worship. David, a shepherd boy who became king, is referred to as the sweet psalmist of Israel because of his understanding of praise and worship ministry.

God's position about David is clear: "After this I will return and will rebuild the tabernacle of David which has fallen down..." (Acts 15:16). This "tabernacle of David" represents, among other things, certain truths about David's understanding of worship forms. God gave to David these insights but, according to the passage, it has "fallen down" (is lost and needs to be restored). God Himself will champion the restoration process of these truths, and this includes worship forms. Throughout Scripture, especially the Psalms, David instructs us how to worship God through various forms. These can be grouped into four main categories.

1. Vocal forms-using the voice, (i.e., singing, shouting, speaking, etc.)

2. Hands-using the hands, (i.e., lifting the hands, clapping, playing musical instruments, etc.)

3. Body postures-using various body postures, (i.e., kneeling, bowing, lying prostrate, standing, dancing, etc.)

4. Other postures-meditating and silently thinking on God, etc.

These can be broken down into more expressions, but these are the primary forms of worship commonly used.

They are not just empty forms but spiritually and scripturally significant for worship. These forms of worship are used throughout Scripture, the most common being standing, bowing and singing. Some of these same worship forms are used in various cultures and other religions. They become meaningful worship when they are presented to God out of a true commitment to Him.

Jesus taught His disciples to pray, "Your will be done on earth as it is in heaven" (Matt. 6:10). Heaven sets the pattern and earth imitates. Heaven decides and earth executes. In everything we do-especially those things we do in an attempt to please God-if we can only duplicate the pattern in heaven, we would have no problem touching God's heart and releasing His blessings.

Heaven's Pattern

Wanting to enrich man's understanding and practice of worship, God gave the apostle John a glimpse of what happens in heaven so we can reproduce it on earth. God designed this revelation to open our eyes to what should constitute true worship, that which is acceptable in His sight and gladdening to His heart. This also explains what David knew and understood about worship.

This is what the apostle John recorded:

> After these things I looked, and behold, a door standing open in heaven. And the first voice which I heard was like a trumpet speaking with me.... Immediately I was in the Spirit; and behold, a throne set in heaven, and One sat on the throne.... The twenty-four elders fall down before Him who sits on the throne and worship Him who lives for ever and ever, and cast their crowns before the throne, saying, "You are worthy, O Lord, to receive glory and honor and power; for You created all things, and by Your will they exist and were created" (Rev. 4:1-2,10-11).

John saw a throne, which clearly denotes kingship, authority, power and dominion. The description he gave of the One who sat on it does not befit any human. The general atmosphere of the throne commanded fear and reverence that would hold any man in awe. The activity of the twenty-four elders helps us understand the spirit of worship expressed in various forms.

First, they worship with a consciousness of the King's presence and before the great throne symbolizing His authority, power and dominion. They fall down, cast their crowns before the throne, and then they verbalized and sang their worship.

The Lord was to receive all this as glory, honor, majesty and power to His name. Forms of worship visibly expressed are symbols that testify of His glory, honor and power, and majesty.

Form 1: Falling Down Before Him

Falling down before someone denotes abject submission to the person. It carries the message of one losing completely his ego, his self. It is like saying, "You can do all you want to me and with me." It is hitting the "rock bottom" of all submission. It is a sign of absolute surrender and yieldedness and conveys the message of total dependency on the person before whom one falls. It says, "I have nowhere to go except to come to you."

The description John gave does not suggest that the twenty-four elders fell down accidentally or in a haphazard manner. They were not forced by circumstances to fall down or were overpowered in doing it. They did it out of choice.

That is the kind of obeisance that comes from deep within, which defies all odds and gives honor to God to whom alone such honor is due. It is also clear that the twenty-four elders fell down not as ritual, nor as a mere form, but were motivated by the spirit of worship, manifesting abject submission and reverence to God. Their spontaneity explains the willingness with which the activity takes place. This spontaneity gives beauty to the worship form-falling down.

When we fall down before God in the spirit of worship, we do not lose consciousness. We are very conscious of what we are doing. We do that out of a knowing of the personality of God before whom we fall. This makes us lose consciousness of unhealthy and unspiritual pride, of self-centeredness, self-righteousness, self-exaltation, self-conceit and all of self that does not truly enthrone the Lord as King and Master.

Form 2: Casting Their Crowns Before Him

The apostle John described the twenty-four elders as clothed in white raiment and having crowns of gold on their heads. Both the white raiment and crowns of gold represent rewards of righteousness and victory, royal power and material blessing. These elders fought the battle of their lives and emerged victorious, so the crowns of gold must mean a lot to them. This elevated and enviable status is sometimes a result of one's own hard work or family heritage. All these, however, were cast before God in worship.

To cast their crowns meant that they had no value in the presence of God as these elders lay prostrate. Casting those crowns said that God is worthy to receive these same crowns for which they had toiled.

The spirit of worship says that in the presence of God, all that one has acquired, achieved, lived for, and is ready to died for belongs to God-and He must have them. One cannot hold onto these things in the presence of God. It means God is more worthy than all these achievements.

All those feats are representations of the creative power of God loaned to the worshiper. A man goes after those things because he cannot perceive and understand God's grace, mercy and gift of life. So the understanding is that if one comes into the presence of God, who gave the best of these achievements, what then becomes the value of these achievements?

This is the spirit of worship that makes casting those crowns before God spontaneous and from the depths of the heart. While bowing down in worship, lying prostrate is itself worship. Giving our time, love and material wealth in service to God's kingdom are all forms of worship that represents the "casting of the crowns of our lives" to God.

If I find Him whom my soul has been earnestly looking for, what is the value of anything I hold in my hands? What is the worth of any decoration on my body? This is the spirit of worship in physical and visible expression.

Form 3: Verbalizing the Spirit of Worship

Jesus said, "Out of the abundance of the heart the mouth speaks" (Matt. 12:34). Anytime the mouth speaks, there can be no doubt about the authenticity of that speech. That is a proclamation of power, a revelation of the individual at that moment in time.

The spirit of worship does not lack words for expression when it comes from deep within. The abundance that gives rise to the verbalizing does not consist of a vacuum. The individual may be overwhelmed by the acknowledgment of God, but the spirit of worship will still find verbal expression in addition to the other expressions mentioned earlier.

> Let the word of Christ dwell in you richly in all wisdom, teaching and admonishing one another in psalms and hymns and spiritual songs, singing with grace in your hearts to the Lord (Col. 3:16).

The above passage tells us that one of the most effec-

43

tive ways to verbalize worship is to feed richly in the Word of God on a daily basis.

Putting It All in Focus

The panorama of Revelation 4 summarizes the three components of worship as defined earlier in our tree model. We can see the base, which is submission and yieldedness to God, flowing in the stem-a truly healthy and spiritual relationship with Him-and then manifested in the fruit, represented by the various forms portrayed.

Under the Old Testament, the Israelites needed to be taught by law. Everything had to be written down for them. Under the New Testament, the liberty of the Holy Spirit helps us to release the hidden potential of worship within us that has not yet been rehearsed.

In view of these, you can do so much. You can express in song what has not been written in the Bible. You can sing a new song that is not known to anyone. That song becomes an expression of your own worship, which the psalmist calls "a new song unto the Lord." New depths of expressions for the New Testament worshiper give him an advantage over the Old Testament worshiper.

When you come to church and lift your hands but do not sing, you are still worshiping. Lifting your hands is still worship even though it indicates only one form of worship. In the New Testament, God wants us to be familiar with all the forms of worship.

You and I can do more than what the people of the

Old Testament did in terms of expressing diverse forms of worship.

Conclusion

As we continue to explore these truths in greater detail, let us emphasize again that one great lack of the church today is a bold, daring exploration of worship forms. There are expressions of worship still locked inside us, waiting to be poured out in worship to God. These forms are His honor, glory, majesty, praise, adoration and thanksgiving. They open the gateway to the presence of God's glory. Let us therefore come into His presence with all of these worship forms in the beauty of His holiness.

5

VERBALIZATION

The primary way a man expresses himself is by speaking. His words-and the way he says them-reveal to a large extent what has been going on inside him. This is one area in worship where our understanding needs to be clarified. It is common to find a believer supposedly worshiping God, or involved in praising and giving thanks to God, repeating the same phrase over and over again. At best, one often finds the believer saying, "I praise You, Lord," "I worship You, Lord," or "We give You all the glory."

After repeating these and similar phrases for a few minutes, some believers just begin to worship in the language of the spirit and use this medium for the rest of the worship time. Later we will talk about worshiping in the language of the spirit, but let us explore verbalizing as a form of worship.

Remember God commands us through the prophet Hosea, "Take words with you, and return to the Lord.... For we will offer the sacrifices of our lips" (Hos. 14:2). The sacrifice of our lips, which is symbolic of and synonymous with worship, is primarily done with words.

The apostle Paul exhorted believers, "Let the word of Christ dwell in you richly in all wisdom, teaching and admonishing one another in psalms and hymns and spiritual songs, singing with grace in your hearts to the Lord" (Col. 3:16).

When you allow the Word to dwell in you richly, it flows out of you. You won't have any problem recounting the awesome attributes of God or His mighty deeds.

Do you know what I find interesting about the various prayers of Old Testament saints? Their verbalized worship attests to their individual experiences with God. What they verbalized was not another person's three-hundred-year-old experience with God, but their own unique experiences. The things they said were not a rehearsal of someone else's verbalized worship. These patriarchs of faith had encountered God for themselves. They spoke and sang His Majesty's worship out of the validity of this experience.

The scenarios we will examine are both words and song (verbalized worship). The same words could be spoken to God as worship without any melody.

Moses' Prayer of Worship

Let's look at Moses' prayer after God delivered His people from slavery in Egypt. The Israelites had been in bondage for over 430 years under the harsh rulership of the Pharaoh who did not know Joseph. In their pain and agony, the Israelites cried to God for deliverance. God heard their cry and sent Moses His servant. After God had taken them out of the land, giving them the hope of liberty, they stood before the Red Sea with the Egyptians pursuing them. God intervened again, and with Moses' rod He brought deliverance to Israel. At the end of the battle, the song Moses sang with the Israelites was a product of the spirit of worship.

The details of that song describe what consumed the Israelites as they were ushered into the joy of deliverance and salvation.

> Then Moses and the children of Israel sang this song to the Lord, and spoke, saying: I will sing to the Lord, for He has triumphed gloriously! The horse and its rider He has thrown into the sea!

> The LORD is my strength and song, and He has become my salvation; He is my God, and I will praise Him; my father's God, and I will exalt Him. The LORD is a man of war: the LORD is His name.

> Pharaoh's chariots and his army He has cast into the sea; his chosen captains also are drowned in the Red Sea. The depths have covered them; they sank to the bottom like a stone.

> Your right hand, O LORD, has become glorious in power. Your right hand, O LORD, has dashed the enemy in pieces. And in the greatness of Your excellence You have overthrown those who rose against You; You sent forth Your wrath which consumed them like stubble.

And with the blast of Your nostrils the waters were gathered together; the floods stood upright like a heap; and the depths congealed in the heart of the sea.

The enemy said, "I will pursue, I will overtake, I will divide the spoil; my desire shall be satisfied on them. I will draw my sword, my hand shall destroy them."

You blew with Your wind, the sea covered them; they sank like lead in the mighty waters.

Who is like You, O LORD, among the gods? Who is like You, glorious in holiness, fearful in praises, doing wonders? You stretched out Your right hand; the earth swallowed them.

You in Your mercy have led forth the people whom You have redeemed; You have guided them in Your strength to Your holy habitation (Exod. 15:1-13).

In this passage, Moses verbalizes God's greatness and identifies Him as his strength and refuge. He also compares God with all who rose against Him and establishes God's superiority over them all. The song contains a rehearsal of the events, a short panorama in which God's greatness is manifest.

If you examine this passage, you will see that it is entirely devoid of common, excessively repetitive phrases such as "We lift You up," "We exalt You," "We give You the glory," and so on. An observer would remark, "These people are praising God. They are giving Him glory. They are thankful to Him." It is our testimony that automatically brings glory to God.

As the Israelites continually recounted the goodness of God by enumerating the things He had done, this ministering was in the spirit of worship but with words. As long as they kept rehearsing these things as a result of their rich experience with God, they were in the spirit of worship but were still using words.

When we verbalize our worship properly, we give adequate expression to what has consumed us, we keep ourselves in His presence. Our faith is kept high as we continue to worship Him. The holy fear of God grips us. All these things make the worship experience very beautiful and fulfilling indeed.

Hannah's Song

Hannah, who was barren, had sought a child from the Lord for years while facing persecution from her rival who had children. When she was so deeply involved in prayer and only her lips could move, she was accused of being drunk with wine. This accusation came from none other than Eli, the high priest. What irony!

Against this background the Lord remembered Hannah and gave her a son. Let's examine Hannah's prayer of worship:

> And Hannah prayed and said: "My heart rejoices in the LORD; my horn is exalted in the LORD. I smile at my enemies, because I rejoice in Your salvation. There is none holy like the LORD, for there is none besides You, nor is there any rock like our God.

"Talk no more so very proudly; let no arrogance come from your mouth, for the LORD is the God of knowledge; and by Him actions are weighed. The bows of the mighty men are broken, and those who stumbled are girded with strength.

"Those who were full have hired themselves out for bread, and those who were hungry have ceased to hunger. Even the barren has borne seven, and she who has many children has become feeble.

"The LORD kills and makes alive; He brings down to the grave and brings up. The LORD makes poor and makes rich; He brings low and lifts up. He raises the poor from the dust and lifts the beggar from the ash heap, to set them among princes and make them inherit the throne of glory. For the pillars of the earth are the LORD'S, and He has set the world upon them.

"He will guard the feet of His saints, but the wicked shall be silent in darkness. For by strength no man shall prevail. The adversaries of the LORD shall be broken in pieces; from heaven He will thunder against them. The Lord will judge the ends of the earth. He will give strength to His king, and exalt the horn of His anointed" (1 Sam. 2:1-10).

Hannah speaks (verbalizes) God's incomparability with none other. She also talks of God's greatness and calls for every mouth to remain shut in God's presence. She speaks of God's sovereignty in deciding what to do with the poor and downtrodden. These words are not only comprehensible to the human mind but also contain enough substance to keep one sober and stunned before the Almighty and just be humbled in His presence. There are no vain repetitions, no following the crowd to rattle what others are saying. These words describe her situation for which God deserved praise and worship. This is truly out of the abundance of the heart and her own experience with God.

Effective verbalizing of worship gets more fulfilling for us depending on how richly we feed on God's Word and how rich our experience with God is! Our experience with God does not depend on how long we have known Him but on how much of God we really have.

The striking feature in these examples of worship is the substance of the verbalization. Why is this important? When words vividly describe a situation that is meant to exalt God and declare the wonders of His name and power, the worshiper is constantly kept in the spirit of worship. In this state all that matters to him is the greatness of God. How often do we rob ourselves of this rich experience by vain repetitions, empty imaginations and a tendency to just start rattling in the prayer language of the spirit, that is, speaking in tongues, instead of properly verbalizing our worship?

The Magnificat

The New Testament records Mary's verbalized worship when she visits Elizabeth. Both cousins found favor in the sight of God, one bearing the forerunner of Jesus and the other, the Messiah Himself. They meet and greet each other. Mary's greeting causes John to leap with joy, and that prompts Elizabeth to call Mary blessed and to prophesy the performance of things spoken to her from the Lord. Now listen to Mary:

My soul magnifies the Lord, and my spirit has rejoiced in God my Savior. For He has regarded the lowly state of His maidservant; for behold, henceforth all generations will call me blessed.

For He who is mighty has done great things for me, and holy is His name. And His mercy is on those who fear Him from generation to generation.

He has shown strength with His arm; He has scattered the proud in the imagination of their hearts. He has put down the mighty from their thrones, and exalted the lowly. He has filled the hungry with good things, and the rich He has sent away empty.

He has helped His servant Israel, in remembrance of His mercy, as He spoke to our fathers, to Abraham and to his seed forever (Luke 1:46-55).

Mary alludes to God's sovereignty and His mercy from generation to generation. Although she does not narrate a lot of incidents, she poetically and beautifully rehearses God's greatness.

You never leave the spirit of worship if the greatness of what God has done continually resides on your lips and in your heart.

Pentecost

Let's look at the event that took place on the day of Pentecost. The great and awesome experience of the baptism of the Holy Spirit with the physical evidence of speaking in the language of the Spirit (tongues) also signifies verbalizing worship and praise of God in a remarkable way.

When the Holy Spirit came, manifesting Himself as God's presence like a mighty rushing wind, the disciples spoke in other tongues as the Holy Spirit gave them utterance.

The multitude marveled, saying they were "speaking in our own tongues the wonderful works of God" (Acts 2:11). They verbalized worship on a totally new spiritual level. They spoke with the language of the Spirit, God's majesty and power, and His greatness.

The bystanders who witnessed this experience, but could not accept its reality for whatever reason, mocked the validity and beauty of this outpouring. They wondered how this whole experience of verbalizing God's worship could be done on such a totally new level of spirituality. Remember the apostle Paul says:

> I will pray with the spirit, and I will also pray with the understanding. I will sing with the spirit, and I will also sing with the understanding (1 Cor. 14:15).

The challenge for us as God's children today is not only to explore all the diverse forms of verbalizing worship (including this one) but also to boldly move into all these depths to enrich our worship experience.

6

SINGING

As humans we sing for leisure, entertainment, for joy and also to express sorrow (typical of African and Asian societies). Singing is an integral part of our socio-cultural activities, even in farming. For example, melody is typical of the normal African daily existence. We hum familiar and unfamiliar tunes when we desire. Singing, music and melody are a part of humanity, and using them as forms of worship to God comes naturally.

We are talking about singing as your personal ministry to God, however. When you sing to God, you use a major expression of worship. Singing, an outstanding form of worship to God, is also the primary form of worship that most adequately brings out from within you all that wants to praise God. Your voice pours out from within more than your hands, feet and other parts of your body do.

If you study the Bible closely, you will notice that singing has always been a major form of worship. In the Book of Psalms, one of the most common forms of worship the Israelites practiced was singing. Today singing has become an important form of worship for the church. Different kinds of singing will enrich our worship life.

Psalm 103:1 reads, "Bless the Lord, O my soul; and all that is within me, bless His holy name." One practical way to bless the Lord with all that is within you is with singing.

> Oh, bless our God, you peoples! And make the voice of His praise to be heard (Ps. 66:8).

> Sing unto the Lord with the harp; with the harp, and the voice of a psalm. (Ps. 98:5).

In other words, use the voice to sing God's praise with the harp (playing instrument) to worship the Lord.

> The voice of rejoicing and salvation is in the tents of the righteous: the right hand of the Lord does valiantly (Ps. 118:15).

The voice of rejoicing also means the voice of singing.

> I will bless the Lord at all times: His praise shall continually be in my mouth (Ps. 34:1).

In all these verses, the psalmist mentions the use of human voice as an important form of worship. In one instance he mentions singing with the harp as well. Furthermore, we can also give "voice" to any psalm, song, or music either with the human voice or other musical instrument. Giving voice in this particular context is giving clear amplification to all the depth of intricate worship within us that is not yet audible.

Healing the Nations With Song

We have barely tapped the potential of how worship can change our lives, our families, our churches and yes-even the nations.

> Thus saith the Lord; Again there shall be heard in this place, which ye say shall be desolate without man and without beast, even in the cities of Judah, and in the streets of Jerusalem, that are desolate, without man, and without inhabitant, and without beast, the voice of joy, and the voice of gladness, the voice of the bridegroom, and the voice of the bride, the voice of them that shall say, Praise the Lord of hosts: for the Lord is good; for his mercy endureth for ever: and of them that shall bring the sacrifice of praise into the house of the Lord. For I will cause to return the captivity of the land, as at the first, saith the Lord (Jer. 33:10-11, KJV).

God's burning desire and promise is that the voice of singing and worship in the celebration of joy and gladness will be heard again in this place that everyone called "desolate without man and without beast." In other words, the principal thing happening will be the restoration of this critical ministry where the voice of singing is used to express God's worship in joy, gladness and praise. This eventually results in "the returning of the captivity of the land"-the healing and emancipation of the land.

God is, therefore, bringing back greater joy of His worship through singing in His presence. As God does this, He will also "return the captivity of the land" just like the former days of glory.

Notice the relationship between the restoration of God's true worship through singing and how that positively affects the healing and restoration of the land. Putting it all together will mean that the true worship of God expressed through singing is critical for the total economic, social, political and spiritual healing of any nation.

I want to declare prophetically that as the church of Jesus Christ enters the twenty-first century, the Holy Spirit is blowing the strongest winds and waves of restoring God's true worship through singing. This will shake and shape for the better the spiritual, political, economic, social and total lives of nations while sweeping them into the kingdom of God.

The prophet Zechariah confirmed this prophetic truth: "And it shall be that whichever of the families of the earth do not come up to Jerusalem to worship the King, the Lord of hosts, on them there will be no rain" (Zech. 14:17).

Today we are commanded to worship God in spirit and truth and not necessarily in a specific physical place. The principal terms and conditions are still the same, however. If the families, peoples, races, colors, tribes and gender of the earth do not worship God, the King of Glory, there will be no "rain" falling on us.

This common phenomenon of the worship of the King will include "the voice of them that shall say, Praise the Lord of host: for the Lord is good; for his mercy endureth for ever: and of them that shall bring the sacrifice of praise into the house of the Lord." All of this exciting work of the Holy Spirit is already the common feature of any gathering of God's people today, but we are yet to witness more exciting developments along this same trend.

Obviously the "rains" of God, according to Zechariah, are not physical rain. The "rain" in this context is the manifested awesome presence of God's glory released on us as a result of our worship. The tangible and manifested clouds of God's glory will release on us the "rains" of His presence, resulting in spiritual, physical and economic fruitfulness in our individual and corporate national lives. Physical rains produce fruitful vegetation. The "rains" of God's presence, because of our singing and worship, also result in a fruitful life.

Voice of Bride and Groom

Our passage in Jeremiah says that there shall be heard again "the voice of the bridegroom, and the voice of the bride." God is restoring the voice of the bride and bridegroom. Who is the bride? The bride is the church of Jesus Christ; you and I who know Jesus Christ both as Lord and Savior and are washed in His precious blood. Our voice is the voice of singing and worship in gladness and joy and praise. It is the lavishing of love, appreciation, adoration and submission to God and the bridegroom. God loves to hear this "voice" again and again. It is being heard but will ring louder and clearer.

The voice of the bridegroom is also that of the Lord Jesus Christ and His Holy Spirit. Whenever you hear the Word of God taught and preached, that is the voice of the bridegroom. The prophetic word of God through His prophets also represents the voice of the bridegroom.

God is bringing back the voice of the bridegroom louder, stronger and clearer to the church bride as she also lifts her voice in love and worship to God and the groom. The Song of Solomon paints a picture of the voice of the church bride to the Lord Jesus Christ, the groom, in lavishing love and worship. The voice of the groom speaks to the church bride with words of comforting exhortation, refreshing words that uplift her. The voice of the church bride in worship releases the voice of the groom. As the voice of the church bride and the Lord Jesus Christ are restored to each other, this will all result in the "returning of the captivity of the land." True worship in God's awesome presence will release the prophetic word of God for the healing of the land. It is happening now!

United Worship through Singing

How do we achieve real corporate worship? Even though you may not know a song, you should still be a part of it. You must lift up your voice and give worship to the Lord.

> Thy watchmen shall lift up the voice; with the voice together shall they sing: for they shall see eye to eye,

when the Lord shall bring again Zion. Break forth into joy, sing together, ye waste places of Jerusalem: for the Lord hath comforted his people, he hath redeemed Jerusalem (Isa. 52:8-9, KJV).

When we come to church, our expectation is to minister to the Lord and that we, in turn, be ministered to. When we do not sing during worship, the worship service is woefully undercut in its fulfilling experience. In enjoying ultimate fulfillment in the worship experience, we are commanded, "...with the voice together ...sing, ...see eye to eye, ...break forth into joy, sing together." This is a graphic display of unity of purpose and understanding in corporate worship. As we sing together, this releases the most rewarding and fulfilling experience in worship. The other implication is that corporate worship thrives in the atmosphere of forgiveness, true love and fellowship. Our worship to God is affected by our relationship with each other.

With the Spirit and Understanding

The apostle Paul wrote, "I will sing with the spirit, and I will also sing with the understanding" (1 Cor. 14:15).

This statement, which we have dealt with previously, begins by explaining what speaking in an unknown tongue is, notably praying with the spirit and singing with the spirit. The passage contrasts praying with the spirit and praying with the understanding, and singing with the spirit and singing with the understanding.

We are commanded to both sing with the spirit and sing with the understanding. This means singing both in the language of the spirit, or in unknown tongues, and also in an intelligible and understandable language to the worshiper. This is indeed a great depth and level of worship that adds a totally new dimension to the worship experience of the child of God.

Singing Aloud

We should also sing aloud. (See Psalms 51:14; 59:16; 81:1; 149:5.) The word aloud has a slightly different meaning from normal English. It is a strident sound, one that is very harsh or shrill, or a shout with joy. This suggests another dimension of giving sound in greater volume and intensity to our worship of singing.

Humming the Song

Other singing forms and creative worship include humming a song to allow for more in-depth concentration and meditation in God's presence. This should intersperse our worship.

Sing of His Righteousness and Mercy

Our singing should be of God's righteousness and judgments. (See Psalms 101:1; 145:7.) These constitute among other things His nature and attributes; His ways, likes and dislikes, and His dealings with mankind. Songs in this regard even include songs that adore His person, thereby deepening our consecration and dedication to Him.

Singing of His mercy, love and majesty should recount His works of mercy, His nature of love and His kingly majesty. (See Psalm 89:1; Isaiah 24:14.)

Songs of Zion

We should also sing "songs of Zion," or songs of the church. (See Psalm 137:3.) Singing about the church and her strength and beauty and peoples is not worship to God but scriptural and proper. These indirectly enrich the worship experience.

With Instruments of Music

Another worship form is singing with instruments of music. David wrote, "On a harp of ten strings I will sing praises to You" (Ps. 144:9). Singing should be interspersed with instruments of music not just in accompaniment, but these instruments must minister in separate ministry of worship to the Lord. Depending on the special nature of a service or the song itself, singing can also be done with a lot more rhythm emphasis. Psalm 149:3 enjoins us to "sing praises to Him with the timbrel [tambourine]" or any other percussive and rhythmic instruments. Singing should be with rhythm, and sometimes rhythm alone is a good worship form.

There are still more diverse forms that the corporate worship leader can take time to prayerfully generate.

Joyful Noise

We can sing while making a joyful noise to the Lord. Singing can sometimes be without intelligibly structured words and melody but with joyful noise. Scripture command us to use this worship form in ministering to the Lord. "Make a joyful noise unto the Lord, all ye lands" (Ps. 100:1, KJV).

Instead of saying something in the song, we can just create a joyful noise with the music.

Voice of Melody

Just making melody is in itself a major worship form. Sometimes we do not just sing or make a joyful noise but use the voice to make melody. The sound of the musical instruments without any words is the melody.

> For the Lord will comfort Zion, He will comfort all her waste places; He will make her wilderness like Eden, and her desert like the garden of the Lord; joy and gladness will be found in it, thanksgiving and the voice of melody (Isa. 51:3).

Sometimes you may be able to tell the song being played even though there are no audible words or structured rhythm. The Bible commands that with the voice we should also make melody. In other words, without words we should use the voice to make melody spontaneously and as inspired by the presence of His glory. As we give to Him worship with the voice of melody, the Lord will bring comforting ministry to Zion (the church), restoring her in full glory and power. He will "make her wilderness like Eden, and her desert like the garden of the Lord," bringing the church into abounding fruitfulness and productivity in every sphere and area of her life. The Lord is already doing this in our lives in various ways we do not fully realize. However, He still expects the return of our gratitude in thanksgiving through the voice of melody.

> Therefore do not be unwise, but understand what the will of the Lord is. And do not be drunk with

wine, in which is dissipation; but be filled with the Spirit, speaking to one another in psalms and hymns and spiritual songs, singing and making melody in your heart to the Lord (Eph. 5:17-19).

We sing, make melody, and make a joyful noise with our voice. For many of us, making melody using the voice may be new. But if we practice it, we will get used to it. All these are forms of worship using the human voice.

The psalmist also said: "All that is within me, bless the Lord." I want you to know that there is so much worship and singing potential within you that you cannot easily express with words alone. Even in human relations, sometimes you love a person so much, when you see that person you just sigh to yourself and cannot say anything. God wants to hear the voice of the bride in all these diverse expressions of love and express worship to Him through singing and melody using the voice.

7

BODY EXPRESSIONS

Psalm 103:1 says, "Bless the Lord, O my soul; and all that is within me, bless His holy name!". "All that is within me" constitutes depths and varied deliberations. There is so much love that the "inside" of a man wants to communicate, but the mouth alone is inadequate to express. Song of Solomon 8:7 refers to love as a force that many waters cannot quench. The body would therefore have to share in expressing all that is within. In our fellowship of love and worship to the Lord, our bodies physically express what the spirit of worship is communicating to the Lord from within us. Where the Spirit of the Lord is there is liberty; therefore we should enjoy spiritual freedom to express holy worship to the Lord.

Any physical posture adopted in worship must truly represent the proper attitude and the spirit of worship before God. The outer must reflect the inner man.

Posture

The physical and body expressions for worship, even as seen in the Bible, are less vibrant in most cases. The commonly used postures are: Bowing the head, bowing from the waist, kneeling, lying prostrate, standing, lifting the hands and standing in deep meditation of God's awesome presence.

In Revelation 4 we see examples of body postures in worship. While the angelic guardians of the throne of God proclaim His holiness, the twenty-four elders cast their crowns (implying use of hands) and fall down.

We may weep and cry (as in Luke 7:36-50) because we are overwhelmed with the extent of God's love, forgiveness and glorious presence.

Let us briefly look at the significance of just a few:

Standing

Standing is another worship form that signifies honor, recognition and a salute. Standing should not always be a command from the worship leader but a willing posture of worship that we are ready to give to the Lord. Standing was a common feature of Israel's worship and other customs. They stood to eat the Passover feast. Standing also suggests a sense of urgency and a readiness for serious business. Standing as a body expression in worship is Scriptural.

Lifting Hands

Lifting the hands is a posture for praise as well as worship. In the Hebrew, it is yada, which is also a yielding, surrender and submission. As children we played "hide and seek." You looked for your partner who was hiding. If you were the first to find him, then he raised his hands in surrender. That made you the winner. Lifting the hands in worship carries the same significance. It says, "I surrender all of my life to You, Lord, because You win over all my arguments." Sometimes we have so many reasons why we cannot worship God the way He wants us to. Lifting our hands tells God, "You win. I will worship You." Let us lift our hands in worship.

Bowing

Bowing is commonly associated with "making obeisance." This is honor, deep respect and reverence. Bowing the head or bowing from the waist says, "I honor You." We honor God when we bow because worship honors Him. Bowing down characterizes the worship of God's people both in the Old and New Testaments.

Abraham's servant bowed his head. "Then the man bowed down his head and worshiped the Lord" (Gen. 24:26).

The assembly of Israel bowed before God. "Then David said to all the congregation, 'Now bless the Lord your God.' So all the congregation blessed the Lord God of their fathers, and bowed their heads and prostrated themselves before the Lord and the king" (1 Chron. 29:20).

Kneeling

Kneeling goes beyond honor into submission. When we kneel, we say, "We submit to You." You cannot submit to a person without submitting to his authority. Your humble position says, "You have the power over me." Psalm 95:6

says, "Let us kneel before the Lord our Maker." Kneeling in worship means you accept God's ownership of you and your belongings. In many churches today people do not often kneel and fall down. The seating arrangement may be such that it is impossible. In some instances people have become too sophisticated to kneel and fall down. Remember that we miss a lot in our worship experience when we do not use all the expressions of worship, including kneeling.

Lying Prostrate

Revelation 4:9-11 shows how the twenty-four elders fall down before God in worship. That is a much deeper level of yielding or abject submission. When we lie prostrate we say to God, "We are ready for utmost obedience and submission." It is like saying you have hit the "rock bottom" of obedience and submission. There is nowhere else to go. You're saying, "You can walk over me because my obedience is complete."

Lying prostrate is establishing God's utmost and un-qualified sovereignty, authority, superiority and worthiness over your insufficiency and unworthiness. It is worship ex-pression at its peak when it is truly from the heart. It takes a lot to demonstrate this worship posture, but God is looking for worshipers of this sort. At this point we are ready to give everything no matter the cost to us.

Meditation

So much goes on within us in worship that cannot adequately be expressed through our bodies. This is nor-mally because of the extremely intense emotion associated with it. The only ways we find to express these (especially in the spirit of worship) are through weeping, crying or in quiet meditation-thinking on God's goodness, mercy and His awesome presence. These expressions sometimes represent the most intense of all that is within, and we must without apologies or reservations release ourselves in these.

The psalmist wrote, "Our fathers in Egypt did not understand Your wonders; they did not remember the multitude of Your mercies ..." (Ps. 106:7). The psalmist noted how casually Israel took God's miracles and mercies. They even took God for granted in all these things. How then could they be consumed with God and His goodness and mercy in worship?

The psalmist says, "But as for me, I will come into Your house in the multitude of Your mercy; in fear of You I will worship toward Your holy temple" (Ps. 5:7). The contrast is striking here. He says, "I will not take You for granted. I will come into Your house to worship, being extremely conscious of Your mercy, and I will worship in holy fear." The result will be a consummation of God's awesome presence by the worshiper to the point where he intensely meditates on God with awe. This should be the mental posture and attitude in worship.

Postures and Levels of Fellowship

Postures used in worship vary, depending on the depth or level of fellowship one may be having with God. Psalm 100:4 describes the progression like this: "Enter into His gates with thanksgiving, and into His courts with praise ..."

The next step after the courts will be the "inner room" where the deepest fellowship takes place; in our context, the deepest worship occurs in God's presence.

Remember, however, that thanksgiving and praise are aspects of the totality of our worship lives. Worship begins with thanksgiving, progresses into praise, and then moves into the depth of worship.

Let us use a house as an example. You enter first through the gate, then you are escorted through the courts (porch or parlor), and then into the inside rooms. In our context, therefore, we say that thanksgiving begins in the "gates" as a lifestyle, before praise in the "courts," then progresses into worship. All three are always done in God's presence, but worship is a more intense fellowship of love with a greater consciousness of His presence.

In the temple worship of the "church in the wilderness" (Israel), the worshipers came with various sacrifices through the gates, then into the courts (through the priests), then into His presence. The high priest took your sacrifices of worship once a year into the holy place on your behalf.

Postures for the different ministries at these levels of fellowship with God varied. The hands and mouth were used primarily in giving thanks, as it is in the Christian church today. Praise progresses with the use of more distinct and vibrant postures because praise by nature is more expressive and extroversive, that is, "openly demonstrated." Praise therefore is energetic and needs the cooperation of the soul. Praise makes an "outward show" of the goodness and glory of God, while worship is introversive, that is, more in-depth communion and fellowship with God. Hence the different postures for worship. In any case, some of the postures used for praise overlap with those for worship. It must, however, be emphasized that worship is the most intense and deep fellowship a man can have with God.

In conclusion, we are commanded in the New Testament to love the Lord our God with all our hearts, minds, souls and strength. This implies worship with our entire body as well.

8

THE CORPORATE
WORSHIP MINISTER

To understand the role of the worship minister, we need to explore God's wisdom in putting people into specific places of function and ability. He is pleased to order and structure the body of Christ that way. He gives every individual his role and function. The gifts or offices differ from one another depending on the specific grace upon each one of us. We must, therefore, discover our place and ability and be pleased to function where God put us.

But now God has set the members, each one of them, in the body just as He pleased.... And God has appointed these in the church: first apostles, second prophets, third teachers, after that miracles, then gifts of healings, helps, administrations, varieties of tongues (1 Cor. 12:18, 28).

For as we have many members in one body, but all the members do not have the same function.... Having then gifts differing according to the grace that is given to us, let us use them: if prophecy, let us prophesy in proportion to our faith; or ministry, let us use it in our ministering: he who teaches, in teaching; he who exhorts, in exhortation; he who gives, with liberality; he who leads, with diligence; he who shows mercy, with cheerfulness. (Rom. 12:4, 6-8).

Gift and Grace

Functioning with any ability in a spiritual office requires a special grace from God, and each man's gift with its grace differs from the other person's gift. The implication is that no one can do exactly what the other does. Even if we appear to possess the same gifts, there will be peculiarities with the manifestation of each man's gift. We are each unique in ourselves and in our places of function and purpose.

The gifts and potential that God put in every man are given names so they also have identity and distinctiveness in their operation. Some of these gifts are apostles, prophets, teachers, miracles, gifts of healings, helps and several others. These gifts and their function differ from each other. The grace of God on each gift will therefore differ one from the other. For example, the pastor or teacher does not have the same grace of God to operate as an evangelist. In the same way neither can the evangelist operate very comfortably as a teacher. Why? Because God gave him the grace to be an evangelist and not a teacher-if he is truly called by God to function in that office of evangelist.

In the same vein, the gift of helps is given to individuals to function in the ministry of helps. According to our passage in Romans, "all the members do not have the same function." That means that not everybody is in the ministry of helps. Taking that one step further, not everyone is graced to be a corporate worship leader. Just as the pastor has a specific grace from God to function as a shepherd, those called into this ministry of helps also have a definite grace from God on their lives to function in this place.

The word help means to support and also to further and contribute to. One who helps does not completely take over, but he does some important things to support and contribute to an already ongoing process. There should therefore be an already ongoing action or activity that will need this specific support and contribution.

The gift, grace, and ministry of helps therefore supports and adds to the total and proper development of the ministry of the local church, its spiritual leadership, and membership.

The Corporate Worship Minister

Functioning as a worship minister is therefore a divine call that comes under the ministry of helps. Like other gifts in the body, it takes a divine calling of God to function in that place. No man can just "jump" into that spiritual office and expect to get the best results. Everybody can worship God, but not everyone can function in that spiritual office of bringing God's people into His presence.

The worship minister has the God-given ability to lead His people in worship. Without his support and contribution, the worship and music ministries may not achieve their full potential. He does not perform the ministry of worship on behalf of the congregation, however, but only lends vital support through his ministry so the individual believer can worship God for himself.

A lot of names or titles have been given to people on whom rests the anointing to lead God's people into His presence. Some call them psalmists, worship leaders, praise leaders, music pastors or music ministers. Whatever title is given them, one way to recognize anyone as a corporate worship minister is that there is always evidence of a greater blessing when he leads the corporate worship and functions in this area of ministry.

An Old Testament Parallel

Let's see if there are any principles of leading worship that we can glean from the following three passages of Scripture.

> And David called for Zadok and Abiathar the priests, and for the Levites: for Uriel, Asaiah, and Joel, Shemaiah, Eliel, and Amminadab.

> Then he said to them, "You are the heads of the fathers' houses of the Levites; sanctify yourselves, you and your brethren, that you may bring up the ark of the Lord God of Israel to the place I have prepared for it. For because you did not do it the first time, the Lord our God broke out against us, because we did not consult Him about the proper order."

> So the priests and the Levites sanctified themselves to bring up the ark of the Lord God of Israel. And the children of the Levites bore the ark of God on their shoulders, by its poles, as Moses had commanded according to the word of the Lord.

Then David spoke to the leaders of the Levites to appoint their brethren to be the singers accompanied by instruments of music, stringed instruments, harps, and cymbals, by raising the voice with resounding joy.

So the Levites appointed Heman the son of Joel; and of his brethren, Asaph the son of Berechiah; and of their brethren, the sons of Merari, Ethan the son of Kushaiah....

The singers, Heman, Asaph, and Ethan, were to sound the cymbals of bronze

(1 Chron. 15:11-17, 19).

Then David gave his son Solomon the plans for the vestibule, its houses, its treasuries, its upper chambers, its inner chambers, and the place of the mercy seat; and the plans for all that he had by the Spirit, of the courts of the house of the Lord, and of all the chambers all round, of the treasuries of the house of God, and of the treasuries for the dedicated things; also for the division of the priests and the Levites, for all the work of the service of the house of the Lord, and for all the articles of service in the house of the Lord (1 Chron. 28:11-13).

And, according to the order of David his father, he [Solomon] appointed the divisions of the priests for their service, the Levites for their duties (to praise and serve before the priests) as the duty of each day required, and the gatekeepers by their divisions at each gate; for so David the man of God had commanded.

They did not depart from the command of the king to the priests and Levites concerning any matter or concerning the treasuries.

Now all the work of Solomon was well-ordered from the day of the foundation of the house of the Lord until it was finished. So the house of the Lord was completed (2 Chron. 8:14-16).

Exegesis on Passages

These three passages also present the same parallel truths in the life of King David as compared with our earlier discussion. A quick glance at the three passages highlights these important points:

- David, having learned a painful lesson that things for God must be done right, summoned the priests concerning this.

- Things had not been done properly; now they must be done after the proper order.

- Part of the proper order was to appoint leaders, including the psalmists and song ministers, so as to give them a sense of leadership duty.

- Before his death, David handed down these principles to his son Solomon.

- These principles, which he had by the Spirit, included the divisions (including schedules and job descriptions) of the priests and all the work of the service of the house of God.

- Solomon did not depart from the commandment of his father David but followed these principles, appointing the worship ministers, musicians, and all the leaders, and the result was that the house of the Lord was completed.

David's life and ministry are not just historical facts; they are symbolic of the life and ministry of the Lord Jesus and also how the church of Jesus Christ will be administered, ordered and structured. According to Revelation 5:5, Jesus Christ, seen by the apostle John as the slain Lamb of God, is the Root of David. This means David's principles of truth sprung from the Spirit of the Lord Jesus Christ.

David considered every responsibility men and women took in the kingdom of God as divinely appointed. This understanding of divine appointment gave everyone who did anything in the house of God a sense of divine call and leadership responsibility.

The "proper order" or proper way of doing things was to appoint men and women into responsibility, so things would be treated with a deep sense of leadership and divine calling. This understanding of doing things was given him by divine inspiration from the Holy Spirit. He also handed down these same principles to his son Solomon. Note the third passage.

All the musicians and those involved in the development of the music ministry and leading the corporate worship had their purposes and schedules clearly spelled out. They knew beyond a shadow of doubt that they had this ministry to dedicate themselves to. They considered it a divine call.

Notice that the overall effect on the house of God was that "the house of the Lord was completed" (2 Chron. 8:16). Completed means not lacking, made ready, peaceable, whole, perfected.

The entire house of God was governed and structured by David on the basis of these principles and truths of divine appointment and call; Solomon, who followed in his father's stead, also enjoyed maturity and wholeness of ministry. This happened because people did not just do things as they pleased but with a sense of call, duty, leadership and appointment.

In other words, there is a completeness and maturity, readiness for God's work, and peace and holiness that characterize the growth of the kingdom of God when people, including worship ministers, take their responsibility in the house of God with a sense of consecration and divine appointment. What's the result? They will do it for God and not for mere human praise. This is the "proper order" that brings completeness and maturity to the entire house of God and its ministry.

Concerning these principles of divine order, this is what God says:

After this I will return and will rebuild the tabernacle of David which has fallen down. I will rebuild its ruins, and I will set it up (Acts 15:16).

According to this passage, God is still interested in the continuity of this truth in the New Testament. Truth never dies. Truth always lives on! These principles of truth in the leadership and administration of King David apply today.

Leading corporate worship constitutes a divine call. It has to be done with a serious sense of leadership responsibility and duty.

Today God is bringing back to the body of Christ an awakening in these areas of truths. There is an awakening concerning true worship and the proper administration of this ministry, including how the leaders should conduct themselves. The fires of this awakening are burning fiercely across the nations of the world because God Himself is blazing this trail. He said, "I will return and ...will rebuild its ruins, and I will set it up." God, the Holy Spirit Himself, is in charge of blazing the new trail of knowledge and understanding.

The Ministry

The corporate worship minister's work is ministry. The word ministry, among other things, means "office or service." As a result of the holy calling and gifting of God to the believer, he automatically receives a ministry. Every believer has a ministry to fulfill. Every genuine ministry has an outstanding quality of a willingness to serve in true meekness and humility.

This should be contrasted with some of the humanistic, perverted understandings of ministry; namely power, position, and the obsession to seize any unhealthy opportunity to reach the top. Ministers must guard against taking undue and unfair advantage of others, amassing wealth just for oneself, and walking in unholy egotism and pride in one's endowment. All these stem from a selfish, self-centered and wrong understanding of ministry. The corporate worship minister should not be identified as such.

True ministry generally involves investing time and energy in others so they can fulfill their God-given purpose. It is usually a position in which one's personal comfort is frequently sacrificed so that other people can achieve God's calling in their own lives.

As worship minister in the church, your work of leading the congregation in worship is ministry or service and, for that matter, a spiritual office. Let's always remember that the office and the gift produce the ministry or service.

The Minister

It is expedient for us to understand a few of the characteristics and expectations of a corporate worship minister.

Anointed and Equipped to Lead

The worship minister leads God's people into His presence. Leading in the corporate praise and worship of the church goes beyond just simply calling out songs sequentially while the congregation follows. This ministry involves things that make the service a greater blessing when that person stands to lead.

The confirmation that a person has been divinely put in this office with the grace to lead is that all are truly refreshed and blessed by his leading and coordinating. The grace to lead makes the whole thing a blessing and refreshing, a joy and full of beauty.

By this one can tell that the worship minister is anointed and graced for this ministry. Almost always everyone desires him to be there to lead the worship, not because of any particular liking for him but because of the blessing he always leaves behind.

In the Old Testament God always commanded that every vessel or tool of ministry be anointed with oil for its specific ministry. Moses built the tabernacle of God after the divine pattern God gave him; among other specific instructions he received was that everything, including all vessels of the tabernacle made for service and ministry, were to have on them holy oil-that was the anointing!

The anointing always meant two things-God's approval and God's supernatural enablement or equipment. That oil literally means God has approved and equipped the vessel for ministry. It also means the vessel has His grace to function according to His purpose. The Old Testament has a unique way of presenting spiritual truths, but this principle is the same in both Old and New Testaments. Anyone God uses must have His supernatural approval and equipment to function, and that is the anointing. It makes the difference!

The worship minister must also learn to equip himself, however. This is through personal discipline to sharpen his leadership and ministry skills, learning to be more imaginative and creative and always desiring to excel in this ministry. (Please refer to 2 Timothy 2:15.) God approves of us as we also study to show ourselves approved.

Coordinator

The worship minister does not worship God on behalf of the people, neither does he directly perform the ministry of worship in their place. In the Old Testament the priest performed some of these sacrifices for and on behalf of the people. In the New Testament context, the individual believer must worship God. All he needs is some help to be able to express more properly his worship.

The worship leader within the context of the New Testament is in this helps ministry to support the development of the corporate worship of the people of God-primarily to coordinate the various activities and details of every praise and worship service. This, therefore, makes him a coordinator, not the "people's worshiper." He guides and coordinates so they can worship God for themselves.

He does this by harmoniously leading the other musicians, the rest of the worship team and the entire congregation. This is what makes the worship leader's work a part of the New Testament ministry of helps. He is a key help in the corporate worship of the church. He is an important coordinator. He should not be self-centered, "doing his own thing," and leaving the rest to reel in confusion. He must be in charge, not in terms of "hijacking" the worship service but by being cooperative and sensitive to all the parts of the entire corporate service.

Prophetic Ministry

The spirit of prophecy is always released more strongly from the spirit of worship. All throughout Scripture, the

ministry of worship and music has always been closely associated with the ministry of the prophetic.

- King David, who was referred to as the sweet
  psalmist of Israel, functioned as a prophet. Some
  of the psalms he wrote are prophecies. His psalmist ministry enhanced the prophetic gift and office.

- Asaph, one of the great psalmists of Israel who also
  wrote some of the psalms, operated as a prophet
  too.

- In 2 Kings 3:15, we see the ministry of the prophet
  in close relation with the ministry of song.

- In 1 Chronicles 25:1-7, we see that in the administration of David concerning song, music, and
  worship, the prophetic ministry was to be a vital
  part of the song and worship ministry.

- Again in Acts 13:2-3, in the atmosphere of praying and fasting and worship (ministering to the
  Lord), prophetic direction for a key missionary
  effort was birthed.

From these and many more case studies in the Scriptures, we see clearly that music, praise and worship have
always provided the atmosphere and platform for the prophetic spirit of God to operate. The worship minister oper-
ates in this arena and atmosphere and, therefore, is a potential prophetic minister. If he develops his praise and worship
ministry well, God, in most cases, increases grace on his life
in this area of prophetic ministry.

Being Knowledgeable

A coordinator must be adequately informed about all the segments he is coordinating so that they can work well together. Imagine someone trying to conduct an orchestra without any knowledge of the instruments and how everything should work together. The whole performance will end up in confusion.

The worship minister must therefore be knowledgeable, well informed, and in tune with all the segments he is coordinating in the corporate worship service. We have already hinted but must emphasize again the need for personal disciplined study, a conscious effort to always upgrade one's knowledge, and a burning desire to excel in this ministry. He should be alert to all aspects of the music of the whole worship service. This means he should be musically knowledgeable and seek to upgrade his knowledge.

Developing Musicianship

A worship leader's ministry is spiritual in nature, but it is also equally important for him to develop his musical skills since music is a major medium in worship. The Bible has much to say about praising and worshiping the Lord with music. Spiritual worship must be expressed with musical skill and excellence. A worship minister is also a music minister and must develop both talents. He must effectively use his music talent as if that's the only means he has to achieve his purpose.

It would be wrong to assume that just because a man is preaching "under the anointing," his mannerisms and other features-including how he communicates with his voice and how he articulates his words-does not really matter because "he is on fire." His audience needs to hear and understand him so faith can be generated for their own encounter with God.

Some Pentecostals and Charismatics wrongly assume that skill doesn't matter in their choir or musical group. Instead they focus on allowing only the words in the song to minister. This is erroneous. For example, before they minister some musical teams say, "Praise the Lord, brothers and sisters. Don't bother too much about the music. Just listen to the words and be blessed." This springs from the belief that music ministry in the church is only a purely spiritual ministry. This is serious error; it is not truth. Music is a primary medium of worship, but it is also an art and a science that must be learned.

God created the medium of music primarily to be used for His worship, and the worship minister must be skillful in this medium. As already stated, music is both art and science, so it must be learned and mastered. Even philosophers consider music the most powerful force of artistry that cuts across race, color, gender, religion, language and other persuasions. Music soothes and lifts the soul. It accentuates and empowers. The worship minister's musicianship cannot be underestimated.

Personal Devotion

This unique ministry of leading praise and worship is directly linked with the worship minister's personal life of sanctity, devotion and Christian conduct. His effectiveness as a worship minister is greatly affected by his lifestyle of personal holiness and continual spiritual growth. Scriptural passages in this chapter already referred to clearly show God's expectations of the holder of any spiritual office.

Men and women anointed to function in any spiritual office have to consider themselves set apart or separated not only to dedicated service to God but to the God of the services. The Old Testament procedure of things pertaining to ministry shows this principle. For example, the high priest had to exemplify holiness, sanctification and devotion by putting on his priestly garments with exact specifications and certain inscriptions on the outer garments. This reminded him that he was set apart for God. His holy lifestyle was a prerequisite for effective ministry.

> "Now take Aaron your brother, and his sons with him, from among the children of Israel, that he may minister to Me as priest, Aaron and Aaron's sons: Nadab, Abihu, Eleazar, and Ithamar.

> "And you shall make holy garments for Aaron your brother, for glory and for beauty.

> "So you shall speak to all who are gifted artisans, whom I have filled with the spirit of wisdom, that they may make Aaron's garments, to sanctify him, that he may minister to Me as priest....

> "You shall also make a plate of pure gold and engrave on it, like the engraving of a signet: HOLINESS TO THE LORD.

> "And you shall put it on a blue cord, that it may be on the turban; it shall be on the front of the turban.

"So it shall be on Aaron's forehead, that Aaron may bear the iniquity of the holy things which the children of Israel hallow in all their holy gifts; and it shall always be on his forehead, that they may be accepted before the LORD" (Exod. 28:1-3, 36-38).

Aaron's ministry would be accepted before the Lord if his commitment to holiness were put on his forehead and made visible to the whole world.

This principle continues in the New Testament. Every member of the body of Christ, graced by God and playing any specific role in the church, functions in the spirit of holiness and sanctity. As the Son of God, Jesus Christ Himself functioned in the principle of personal holiness and as the High Priest of the New Testament.

Concerning His Son Jesus Christ our Lord, who was born of the seed of David according to the flesh, and declared to be the Son of God with power, according to the Spirit of holiness, by the resurrection from the dead
(Rom. 1:3-4).

The New Testament commands believers who have also been made priests to follow His example of ministry.

Take My yoke upon you and learn from Me, for I am gentle and lowly in heart, and you will find rest for your souls (Matt. 11:29).

Without strong dedication and commitment to personal holiness and sanctity, the spiritual ministry, which constitutes the gift and the grace, will be ineffective and will gradually lose favor with God and men.

In King Solomon's era, as every song minister and worship leader stood in this office with the needed understanding, dedication and commitment, the whole community of believers experienced the glory of God as they were gathered in worship. (See 2 Chronicles 5:11-14.) The full glory of God is manifested when men and women see their responsibility in the church as God's sacred appointment and dedicate themselves to it with all seriousness.

Some men and women in the church of Jesus Christ today, who are standing in the congregation, should be leading the worship. Let's get them on the platform where they belong. Some who are called to lead the congregation into God's presence treat this holy office as a hobby. Let me admonish them: It is a holy and divine call!

May all who should stand in this place of ministry begin to function so that the prophetic words of the psalmist, which say that worship will rise to God from the nations, will become a greater reality today.

9

THE CORPORATE WORSHIP SERVICE

The setting where we can see the spirit of true worship and its many forms is the corporate worship service. Whenever the children of God gather, worship is a fundamental feature. Without it, the meeting is short of the total blessing of God. It is the moment when the saints render corporately all that is in their hearts to God in praise and worship. Corporate worship, or the worship service, represents the forum or gathering of the saints of God to offer praise and worship to God.

This practice has its origins as far back as Old Testament history when the leaders of Israel called for an assembly of all the people. Although some of the gatherings were not solely for worship, worship nonetheless was a regular feature.

Surely the righteous shall give thanks to Your name;
the upright shall dwell in Your presence (Ps. 140:13).

I went with them to the house of God, with the voice of joy and praise, with a multitude that kept a pilgrim feast (Ps. 42:4).

From these verses we can deduce that the righteous, or God's people, enjoy God's presence as a result of the corporate ministry of thanksgiving, praise and worship.

The forms of the worship service in the Old Testament were not the same as in the New Testament. Nevertheless, the principles are the same. A people who have experienced the goodness of their God are ready to pour out their hearts to Him in whatever way possible.

A congregation and a team of song ministers, including the corporate worship minister, commonly characterize the worship service. The congregation is ready to worship, and the worship minister helps the congregation get to the throne of God.

The service basically involves the congregation responding positively to the leading of the worship minister and the rest of the team until all are overwhelmed with a strong spirit of worship. Once we get into the spirit of worship and abide there, we begin to enjoy the presence of God with us. That is the essence of our gathering anyway. A meeting of the saints of God, without the tangible presence of God, is like any other social gathering or a religious benevolent society.

When we minister to God in worship, He responds by manifesting His presence.

Bringing All Along

Bringing all along primarily involves helping every member of the congregation to move into the spirit of worship. Once this is done, every member is in a position to touch God and be ministered to by Him in various ways.

A leader always needs to bring everybody along, as much as possible, in any worship service. The spiritual maturity and understanding of the ministry of worship will differ from individual to individual. No worship minister has a perfect situation. No group of believers anywhere possess the same levels of spiritual maturity, understanding and even stamina when worshiping. Some unspiritual people may be present in the praise or worship service.

The worship minister needs to know this so he will not "drive" them along but lead them. Driving the corporate worship service does not bring all along. As stated in Isaiah 40:11, "He will feed His flock like a shepherd; He will gather the lambs with His arm, and carry them in His bosom, and gently lead those who are with young."

In the same fashion that God leads us, so the worship minister also "gently leads" and "gathers with his arm" God's people into His presence, indicating a diversified and creative approach to leading the corporate worship service. In addition to this, the worshipers' personal experiences throughout the week differ. Some may have had pleasant experiences in life, some bitter, some nothing spectacular. All these affect their disposition to the worship service. This leaves the worship minister and the team with a heavy task, especially in a very large congregation. He will have to bring this "mixed multitude" to the experience of fruitful and refreshing worship. That's why he needs a sensitive, diversified and creative approach to the corporate worship service.

Instructing for some short time before any praise or worship service is vital for the development of corporate worship. It helps to effectively lead and bring everybody along.

The teaching should be well tailored, systematic, properly planned, short, precise and specific. This teaching, coupled with a little "tugging" them along with more songs, helps the worship minister to "carry the feeble in his bosom" into God's presence. Some church members may not be used to standing for too long. The most important thing is to get people to truly worship and not just to go through the routine or to drive people through the corporate worship service.

More Than a Prelude

When we minister to God and He ministers to us, the worship service keeps worshipers humble. This phenomenon invariably makes them receptive to God's Word. This should not be the leader's main objective, however. The worship leader's ministry is not just to prepare the congregation to receive the preaching. This may wrongly make people see the corporate worship service as a preliminary item on the church program, leading to a "main feature." God also receives worship as a "main meal" from His children. He gives us His Word. What does He get in return from us? Worship.

If worshipers see worship as a "prelude" to a "main item," subconsciously they may not expect much from the worship service. They may only wait for that to end so they can have the "real thing," which is the Word. During the worship service they may expect only a warm feeling and not a real encounter with God. Through this erroneous impression God's people have been robbed of a true worship experience.

> You have not bought Me the sheep for your burnt offerings, nor have you honored Me with your sacrifices. I have not caused you to serve with grain offerings, nor wearied you with incense. You have bought Me no sweet cane with money, nor have you satisfied Me with the fat of your sacrifices; but you have burdened Me with your sins, you have wearied Me with your iniquities. (Isa. 43:23-24)

God's complaints concerning His people in Isaiah's day are the same for His church today. Instead of bringing "the sheep for your burnt offerings ...your sacrifices ...offerings ...with incense," we have rather brought Him "...no sweet cane with money ...nor have [we] satisfied [Him] with the fat of [our] sacrifices ..." Instead God says to us, "You have burdened Me with your sins [and] wearied Me with your iniquities."

What does that mean? We've been at the receiving end and constantly put God at the giving end-always making God the one to forgive, heal, deliver, restore, nurture, nourish and feed while perfecting us with His Word. This imbalance produces a serious error in our relationship with God, resulting in little and sometimes meaningless worship or no worship at all.

Finally, the worship leader's ministry involves helping the congregation present their thanksgiving, praises and worship to God in an acceptable way. He has the task of helping the congregation stay in the spirit of worship, as described earlier, so much that God will be left with only one option: to "come down and feast" with His beloved children.

Skillful and Creative Worship

Worship, because it is the believer's personal and individual ministry to God, must not be done "just anyhow." Whether on the personal or corporate level, it must be creative and skillful.

> Sing to Him a new song; play skillfully with a shout of joy (Ps. 33:3).

God's Word commands us that the Lord's song must be new and skillful. It takes creative, imaginative minds with skill to bring new ideas into our worship. For our worship, therefore, God's desire is direct: Sing to the Lord a new song and play skillfully. Not the same old songs in the same old lousy, unskilled manner. Bring before God new songs in refreshing ways.

It is more challenging to change the repertoire of the church's worship and come up with new songs in new ways. It doesn't take much effort to sing and worship the way we did ten years ago. It takes greater effort to bring our corporate worship week after week in more skillful and creative ways. Let us therefore challenge ourselves to be more creative, imaginative and skillful in our worship to God.

We must express ourselves to Him in speaking, singing new songs, shouting or making a joyful noise. When appropriate, we may also fall silent in His presence to listen.

We also express ourselves in worship through the use of our hands. We may clap, lift our hands, wave them or play some sort of musical instrument. Finally, we can use our whole body. One may stand, kneel, bow, dance or fall prostrate before God's glory. We participate in such activities based on our understanding of God to whom we ascribe our worship.

We need to create a liberating atmosphere where every individual can freely express the worship that is within him.

The potential beauty of the worship service is manifest when every member, out of the abundance of the spirit of worship within, spontaneously expresses worship in whatever form. When the worship leader has to give instructions at almost every point as to how people should express worship, this indicates the unreadiness and lack of skillful development of the worshiper.

Sensitivity to the Holy Spirit

The worship minister in the corporate worship service should always function in this place of ministry with utmost sensitivity to the Holy Spirit. Romans 8:14 says, "For as many as are led by the Spirit of God, these are sons of God."

First, he must understand the vital role the Holy Spirit plays in making our worship full of spiritual vigor. He is the only Great Teacher of all truth who is the real key help in the development of the corporate worship of the church. Apart from the Holy Spirit bringing illumination to us and guiding our worship in various ways, He also makes the glorious presence of God real. The Holy Spirit will also glorify the Father. He understands perfect worship to God and knows how to help the worship minister fulfill his leading role in a refreshing corporate worship service.

> However, when He, the Spirit of truth, has come, He will guide you into all truth; for He will not speak on His own authority.... He will glorify Me, for He will take of what is Mine and declare it to you (John 16:13a-14).

Being sensitive to the Holy Spirit means letting your intuition become sharp enough to receive instruction from the Lord. It may be that He wants the worshipers to sing a particular song at a certain point, but it's not on your original song list. He may want everyone to keep silent so He can take over the service and deal directly with the worshipers.

Sensitivity to the Holy Spirit is a way of life the worship minister must develop and not a style he just "slots in" during the service. This is a lifelong learning process. Ongoing cultivation of a receptivity to the Holy Spirit becomes a great asset in leading worship. Without it, he leads the congregation through a long session of singing to excite the emotions-not to minister to the Lord.

Tips On How to Lead a Worship Service

The worship service is the believer's total ministry to the Lord. To effectively lead such a service, you first must understand the purpose of the meeting. Then you can proceed to other things such as:

- Always have a freshly updated master list of songs or repertoire that you work with.

- Plan the corporate praise, thanksgiving or worship service as part of the whole meeting by first understanding its theme, purpose and direction.

- Plan the format, beginning with thanksgiving, then praise, and finally worship. Prayerfully plan every detail within the time allotted to you by your pastor or appropriate authority.

- You can begin and close your format with some songs that relate to the general theme and direction of that particular meeting and also songs that are uplifting, refreshing and faith-building. Include a series or sequence of songs that build a sense of unity in worship. Remember these do not necessarily have to be thanksgiving, praise or worship songs.

- Then proceed to select songs specifically for thanksgiving, praise and worship for the service. The words of the song determine whether it is thanksgiving, praise or worship.

- Encourage the congregation at certain points to meditate and reflect on God and the lyrics, especially His awesomeness and goodness. Learn to listen to the Holy Spirit by allowing room for flexibility, innovation and personal expression of worship.

- Avoid the mistake of preaching before and after each song.

- Don't be too lengthy in the worship service if your people are not accustomed to it. This causes weariness of soul and often misses the point of the service-a refreshing encounter with God's presence. Take them one step at a time.

- Don't be afraid to deal with problems-distracting behaviors, unedifying prophecies, show of casual attitudes and disrespect for God's presence, very late arrivals to participate in the worship service, etc.

Extra Advice

- Be adventurous, open to the Holy Spirit, flexible and sensitive at all times.

- Exalt Christ through songs, message and appeal.

- Make each person face the claims of the Lord Jesus Christ.

- Allow room for the Holy Spirit to bring the people to repentance and commitment.

- Pray for the release of the power of God and His blessings upon the service.

- As the leader, you must do all you can to avoid meaningless repetition of songs. If you tire during the course of the service, call on another for help. Avoid repeating choruses to the point where the climax is lost and anything distracts or disrupts the service.

All these tips do not by any means offer a full-proof guarantee for the best worship service. They are only guidelines. You must be prayerful and innovative, looking at your special circumstances. Other helpful hints:

- The worshiper must recognize the importance of songs. Some songs enthrone God and delight Him; others He detests. This is simply because those songs do not testify to the full truth and revelation of who He is and what He represents.

- The worship leader and team should choose songs carefully and consider the melody and its familiarity to all present for the corporate worship service.

- It is very helpful when all appropriate songs express the right mood, spirit and occasion at every point in the service, i.e. a specific song at a particular climax of the worship service can either kill or help the spirit of the service.

- Consider the rhythm that is most appropriate for a specific worship song during the time of ministering to the Lord.

- Analyze the words of the music and be sure they

suit the theme and are scriptural. John 4:24 commands us to worship in truth. John 17:17 says, "Your word is truth." Some songs don't represent the truth of God's Word.

- The worship minister must be careful not to use music forms merely as "ice breakers or time fillers." We do not sing to while away time as we wait for the pastor or preacher for the day. Nor should songs be used as a means of entertainment during the worship.

- The music must focus on God. It must be used to reflect God's glory and honor. Scripture, when sung, is as powerful as the preached Word of God; therefore we must at any given time tap its full potential.

- The worship minister may make use of other voices, such as a worship team, a choir, other soloists or lead singers, accompaniments of piano, guitars, drums and other musical instruments.

- Rehearsal with the entire team before any worship or praise service is always vital. He must not direct undue attention on the musical instruments but on the Lord.

10

THE PRESENCE
OF THE LORD

The Scriptures have established that God is Spirit. Since the human eye can't see Him, one way of "seeing" God has to be a physical manifestation of some sort. The greatest expression of God that is most readily available to us is creation. When God created, He was revealed. We understand His attributes through the things He created. When God became displeased with the way men were living, however, the only way to tell them what He expected was to send His Son Jesus Christ. Jesus' presence settled all the ambiguity about the reality and existence of God as Creator. The most obvious evidence of God's presence in a place or situation is the tangible impression He leaves behind.

Having established that the spirit of worship originates from man toward God, the best illustration we can give to the presence of the Lord is God's response to the spirit of worship. Anytime God sees the spirit of worship, it is like a "container" that has been created for Him to dwell there.

The literal or tangible presence of the Lord manifested in our worship is a result of the active work of the Holy Spirit today. Jesus said that when the Spirit of truth comes, "He will not speak on His own authority, but whatever He hears He will speak" (John 16:13). Verse 14 says, "He will glorify Me, for He will take of what is Mine and declare it to you."

Among all that the Holy Spirit does, He shows us the reality of the things of God and exemplifies God. He shows us what God's glory and presence are like. This is part of the work of glorifying God. As we glorify God in worship, the Holy Spirit teaches us how to do it so we will experience God's presence.

When Jesus left the Father's right hand in heaven, He promised that the Holy Spirit, the third Person in the Godhead, would represent the Godhead here on earth. The Holy Spirit exemplifies the glory of God, His presence and attributes. Wherever He is, God's presence is there.

In Acts 13:2, certain prophets and teachers, while ministering to the Lord, experienced God's presence in worship. We know this because the Holy Spirit spoke concerning a great missionary work for which He had set apart Paul and Barnabas. Where God's presence is, His voice is there as well.

More references to the presence of the Lord in the congregation are found throughout the Scriptures, but let's look at just one such experience.

> And it came to pass, when the priests were come out of the holy place: (for all the priests that were present were sanctified, and did not then wait by course:

Also the Levites which were the singers, all of them
of Asaph, of Heman, of Jeduthun, with their sons
and their brethren, being arrayed in white linen, having cymbals and psalteries and harps, stood at the
east end of the altar, and with them an hundred and
twenty priests sounding with trumpets:)

And it came even to pass, as the trumpeters and singers were as one, to make one sound to be heard in
praising and thanking the Lord; and when they lifted
up their voice with the trumpets and cymbals and
instruments of musick, and praised the Lord, saying, For he is good; for his mercy endureth for ever:
that then the house was filled with a cloud, even the
house of the Lord; so that the priests could not stand
to minister by reason of the cloud: for the glory of
the Lord had filled the house of God
(2 Chron. 5:11-14, KJV).

In this passage, the confirmation of God's presence
was seen in: (1) The house was filled with a cloud; (2) The
priests could no longer stand to minister.

The passage did not describe the posture of the priests,
but it was clear that their bodies gave way. The literal, tangible and manifested glory of God was in the house because
of their worship. Because they had unity of purpose in what
they did, they also enjoyed unity in their understanding as
they worshiped God with singing, melody and instruments
of music. The Bible said they all lifted their voices to the
Lord. While they cried out in one accord, the house was
filled with a cloud-the manifested and literal presence of God.

To Israel the cloud symbolized the tangible presence
of God. In the wilderness it was a pillar of cloud by day, a

pillar of fire by night. In the congregation of Israel it was simply the Lord in the cloud filling the house. Regardless of the form in which this took place, one thing stood clear: it was the supernatural manifestation of God's presence and glory.

What happened with Israel's experience with the presence of the Lord are not things that the human mind can very easily understand and explain.

God has always looked for the opportunity to show His power and glory in the gathering of His people. He has always sought for an opportunity to "be present" in the congregation of the righteous. Our fellowship of love with God in worship has always been the key forum and primary gateway into His presence.

It wasn't just the cloud or the fire that established God's presence. What happened under the cloud also confirmed God's presence. Moses understood this. He wrestled with God when Israel needed the presence of God to enable them to move forward. (See Exodus 33:12-14, 18.)

Evidence of God's Presence

Many things happen whenever we worship. When the presence of God fills our worship, there are healings, diverse breakthroughs and miracles. Sometimes people fall under the power of God. There could also be other manifestations, prophecies, deliverance from curses, emotional healings and other mighty signs and wonders.

The presence of God gives us victory over the enemy. The glory of God's presence does not "come down" at the time of worship for nothing. God's glory is always manifested to minister to the needs of His people. He visits to strengthen, bless, and protect His people. Inasmuch as the presence of God has all these benefits for His people, God also sees that He leads His children into victory over the enemy.

In Psalm 100:2, we are commanded to "come before His presence with singing." According to Psalm 22:3, God inhabits our praises.

The presence of the Lord is the ultimate reason for our worship. We fellowship with God in worship to encounter and enjoy His presence. Anything short of this just makes our worship a routine. The ultimate reason for our gathering to worship should always be because of Him. He is the only reason we are alive-not to please ourselves but Him alone. When His presence is really manifested in our worship, we will feel Him, encounter Him and know Him. This is the essence of worship.

The apostle Paul declared how the unbeliever will encounter God when he comes into the atmosphere of worship, seeing the diverse manifestations of the Holy Spirit. (See 1 Corinthians 14:22-25.)

During the days of King Jehoshaphat, God intervened and ambushed his enemies (the Moabites and Ammonites) and led His people into victory as they worshiped God. (See 2 Chronicles 20:1-30.) The evidence of God's presence was that their enemies destroyed each other and Israel won the victory without a fight. All Israel did was worship Almighty God.

Signs and wonders are manifestations of God's presence. When the apostle Paul and Silas were imprisoned, the Bible says:

> But at midnight Paul and Silas were praying and singing hymns to God, and the prisoners were listening to them. Suddenly there was a great earthquake, so that the foundations of the prison were shaken; and immediately all the doors were opened and everyone's chains were loosed (Acts 16:25-26).

As they chose the path of praise, prayer and worship, this resulted in a violent earthquake that opened the prison doors and loosed their chains. The Scriptures did not categorically say the apostles were asking God to intervene to save them from prison, as was the case when Peter was put in prison. They were just worshiping God, and His presence came to consume their praise. In the process they received release from prison!

Ideally, at the point when God's presence is manifested in corporate worship, the worship leader's presence is no longer needed. Nevertheless, for lack of adequate readiness on the part of most worshipers, they are unable to flow with the Holy Spirit. So, the worship minister often continues to interfere by giving more instructions. I counsel the worship minister to "pull back" and listen to the Holy Spirit's instructions. Allow the Lord's presence for that period to deal with His people according to His mercies.

That explains the situation where the spirit of worship leads you to fall on your face but the worship minister interrupts the flow and says, "Let's rise on our feet." You may feel prompted to kneel, but he says, "Let's lift up our hands."

When the worshiper is in a deep encounter with God, he should have the liberty to continue in whatever posture he finds himself in the communion of the Holy Spirit-unless the worship minister feels strongly impressed by the Holy Spirit to emphasize a different direction or to bring the worship service to an end.

The direction of the spirit of worship in response to the Holy Spirit is the most relevant experience the true worshiper must seek. This is the true worship experience.

This tangible and great glory of God is always experienced in corporate ministry to the Lord. A personal anointing releases a certain measure of God's presence and glory, but the greatest glory is always released in the corporate forum of worship.

Psalm 133 says that God commands "the blessing" where the "brethren ...dwell together in unity." That is what Solomon's gathering in 2 Chronicles 5 was about. When there is unity in worship, the tangible glory of God's presence is released for blessing.

Grieving God's Presence

We can do several things to grieve God's presence. Doing things for display and mere showmanship, which is carnal and unspiritual, grieves God's presence. Pastors and other spiritual leaders, including worship ministers, should not do things to exalt themselves. God's presence is grieved when people in spiritual ministry want to impress and not truly glorify God. When God's presence is grieved, His glory and power are not manifested, and there is no blessing.

Strife, bickering, backbiting and sin in a congregation also grieve God's presence. The apostle Paul said, "Let all things be done decently and in order" (1 Cor. 14:40). Decency and orderliness in a spiritual gathering is key to experiencing God's glory. People are at liberty to prophesy and operate in other gifts of the Holy Spirit, but all should be done decently, orderly and for the true glory of Christ. It should not be difficult to discern between what is truly spiritual and done to the glory of God and what is carnal. If too much of the human self is prevalent in our worship, we must pursue the path of sound spiritual judgment. The Bible gives the spiritually mature the mandate to judge (weigh, investigate, scrutinize) all things. (See 1 Corinthians 2:15.) Even in God's presence, excesses sometimes occur that need to be judged.

God is so real and dwells close to us. The apostle Paul said that our bodies are "the temple of the Holy Spirit" (1 Cor. 6:19). Throughout the Scriptures we have evidence of God's presence near us and in us. Why then do God's people have difficulty in experiencing and enjoying His presence? This is mainly because we do not live daily in the consciousness of God's presence. We are more conscious of what we can see, feel, smell, touch, hear and taste than we are of God's presence living with us and in us.

God can be more real than our physical senses-if through faith in His Word, we totally accept this truth. Any truth we accept, we must also practice. This brings us to the crucial importance of practicing an awareness of God's presence. We must learn to live daily in the consciousness of God's presence. Then worshiping God "in spirit and in truth" will naturally become part of us.

The greatest and most important need in the life of mankind today is God's presence and His tangible glory. The psalmist said, "A day in Your courts [where Your presence is] is better than a thousand. I would rather be a doorkeeper in the house of my God than dwell in the tents of wickedness" (Ps. 84:10). Whatever we do as Christians, we should seek God's presence. We should hunger and thirst for Him above everything else so His presence will fill our whole lives.

> O God, You are my God; early will I seek You; my soul thirsts for You; my flesh longs for You in a dry and thirsty land where there is no water. So I have looked for You in the sanctuary, to see Your power and Your glory (Ps. 63:1-2).

Our desire and passion should be to seek God just to "see His power and His glory." As the human race cries for answers to the many questions arising out of the depravity and sorrow of this generation, the answers are in God's presence and His glory. As a matter of urgency, we must look for God's glorious presence. This is where all the answers are-in His presence.

11

WORSHIP AS A LIFESTYLE

You may think of worship only in terms of a gath ering of the saints characterized by good music led by a leader who brings everyone along into the presence of God. You may think of worship as those isolated moments when you wake up, enter your prayer closet and sing praises to God, telling Him how much you love Him. That still falls short of a lifestyle of worship, however. To help us fully understand this subject, let us examine David's words:

> I will bless the Lord at all times; His praise shall continually be in my mouth (Ps. 34:1).

This introduction to Psalm 34 summarizes the whole subject of worship as a lifestyle. The word bless means "worship." "At all times" and "continually" take worship beyond the walls of the chapel, beyond the congregation of the righteous, and beyond the walls of your closet into the "open," where most of your life is lived.

This is where those whose emphasis in worship lies strongly in the forms will have a problem. How odd would you look if you lifted up your hands in surrender before a job interview? What would the hostess say if you prostrated yourself in worship before a dinner party? What would a doctor think if he heard you singing praises in the examination room?

A lifestyle of worship means worshiping God everywhere. Now "everywhere" means everywhere and "at all times" means at all times. No place is excluded and no time is omitted. The only way it becomes possible to make worship a lifestyle is through conducting all the affairs of our lives in the spirit of worship and maintaining the attitude of worship whenever we may be.

Seeing God in Creation

The psalmist wrote the following:

The heavens declare the glory of God; and the firmament shows His handiwork. Day unto day utters speech, and night unto night reveals knowledge (Ps. 19:1-2).

The apostle Paul, speaking by the Holy Spirit, confirmed this in a passage we quoted earlier:

Because what may be known of God is manifest in them, for God has shown it to them. For since the creation of the world His invisible attributes are clearly seen, being understood by the things that are made (Rom. 1:19-20).

One great observation is that in spite of the environmental degradation and all we have done to destroy God's creation, it is a beautiful world. One does not need to tour the whole world to see the beauty of God's creation. When David made the above declaration, he had not toured the world. He just looked around himself.

The diversity in creation, which we often take for granted, is a good source of God's praise and worship. If you lived in a third world country where the prime concern of men's hearts is how to break the poverty cycle, it might be easy for you to despise the valuable things with which God has blessed us. He intends that all those things, in their small ways, should draw our attention to Him and open our hearts to appreciate Him.

Have you ever driven past a house where the exterior had been beautifully decorated, but you rushed past it because your business partner was waiting? Worse yet, you reached your destination and discovered the individual didn't turn up. You probably left the place disappointed, frustrated and confused. On your way back, you drove past the same house with the beautiful flowers, still in a hurry, never taking time to admire it.

You missed it twice. You missed your business partner and you also missed a good opportunity to admire God's creation. I do not mean for you to stop for five minutes and admire the flowers. Remember that in our quest to make money, money cannot be the only thing on earth.

Countless opportunities in life are meant to draw our attention to God and inspire or rekindle our faith and commitment to Him. All too often, we let these moments pass us by. If we seize them, however, they will invite God's presence into our lives and situations. Unfortunately, we throw away most of these opportunities to allow the beauty of creation to draw out from us the worship of God.

In his quest to look for God in everything, King David turned inward and proclaimed:

> I will praise You, for I am fearfully and wonderfully made: marvelous are Your works, and that my soul knows very well (Ps. 139:14).

Now your body is one thing you carry everywhere. Have you ever meditated on the perfect coordination between the different members of your body? This explains why David proclaimed, "I will bless the Lord at all times."

That kind of worship does not come from the external, and that is what makes it powerful. What comes from within is more powerful than what comes from without.

I believe King David wrote the psalm not just because he had a talent in writing or a flare for music. Many people with tremendous musical talent and poetic skills write on many different things. There is every reason to believe that the spirit of worship motivated King David, which was clearly a lifestyle for this man "after God's heart." Anytime, anywhere, King David was conscious of the presence of God and his heart was open to God's greatness.

What happens in your heart when you see a manifestation of great talents by people around you? When you hear of great achievements, does it immediately register in your heart that God is filling the earth with His goodness through a mortal? When you hear of a near-fatal accident in which nobody died, does it immediately spark gratitude in your heart to God for saving people, or do you spend all the time talking about the devil wanting human blood?

In every life situation, if we have a heart toward God, we find opportunity to say, "Thank You, Jesus!" Within every opportunity, we see the need to worship God.

A Life of Gratitude

A lifestyle of worship is one devoid of complaining, grumbling and any attitude that leaves us cursing the day we were born. When Israel murmured in the wilderness, they paid a high price for it. The Bible says, "For many of them God was not pleased and so He swore in His wrath that they should not enter into His promise."

How easily the child of God joins the rest of the world in giving glory to the devil and elevating Satan over God. Remember that verbalization springs from the abundance of our hearts. We may not open our mouths and curse God, or say anything that obviously displeases God, but our attitudes may speak much more. If you find a saint who comes from church only to complain about everything, you know he sees God as confined to the gathering of the saints. To such a person, the congregation of the righteous appears to be the only place to say "nice things" to God. After the church meeting is over, there is nothing much to thank and worship God for except to wait until the next church service.

Incidentally, we often forget that our attitudes determine the quality of our experience of worship when we gather with other believers. This is vital to note.

A believer who has formed the habit of grumbling and complaining at every opportunity obviously has nothing to meditate on and enjoy in his personal or corporate worship. The saints of old always had reason to praise God and worship Him because they had a lifestyle of continually counting their blessings and rejoice in the goodness of God.

If you go through the school day as a student, the work week as a laborer, or through family issues as a dedicated parent-and you maintain a positive attitude in spite of the "ups and downs" of life-you cultivate a healthy, joyous lifestyle of worship. When you join the saints and sing, "We bring the sacrifice of praise into the house of the Lord," you will easily have worship to offer to the Lord.

We do not come to church to conjure the spirit of worship when it gets to that "item" on the "program." We come to the house of God already prepared with hearts of worship. The psalmist wrote, "Enter into His gates with thanksgiving, and into His courts with praise" (Ps. 100:4).

Many have tried to explain this to mean outer and inner temple and a whole lot of other interpretations. If we look at the person who wrote this, we would get the context right. David had great reverence for God and a lifestyle of gratitude. Anytime he entered the house of God, he already had with him the sacrifice of praise. He already had a thankful heart. He did not need long hours of prompting by a worship minister to get into the spirit of worship. Many of us come to church to receive from God and not to give to Him. If we have this mentality, we will go home without having experienced true worship. Worship is entirely giving from our perspective. If we develop the attitude that a church service involves both giving to God as well as receiving from Him, then throughout the week, we would be assembling what to give to God. In that spirit, counting our blessings becomes a lifestyle.

If we recounted what God has done for us and how good He has been to us during a particular week, that would take us less than one minute. This may not be because God has done nothing good for us. It may be because we don't see His interventions in the small, natural, even mundane issues that we face daily.

Can we say with the songwriter:

He keeps me singing a happy song

He keeps me singing it all day long.

Although the days may be drear He always is near

And that's why my heart is always filled with song

I am singing, singing all day long.

Can we picture an angel placed at the gate of any chapel, inspecting men's hearts and pockets to see the kind of worship and gratitude they have brought to the Lord?

Is it possible for the church to have a culture of presenting our hearts and substance to the Lord in a continual lifestyle of worship? In other words, can all our members understand that church is a primary gathering to count our blessings and be thankful to God in worship? Wouldn't that help people develop a constant expectation of God's visitation in their lives and a reciprocal attitude of thanksgiving and worship to Him?

Conclusion

A true, fulfilling worship experience starts with the individual's understanding that it all begins and ends with him (the worshiper). It is a never-ending, daily, and ongoing ministry to the Lord, whether alone or wherever we may be. The beauty of God's creation, the goodness of the Lord that we enjoy, and all the little things that point to God's mercy are enough worship material to trigger the spirit of worship in our hearts. After all, in heaven this will be our never-ending and eternal ministry to God, which we will timelessly and tirelessly carry out.

Let's begin this lifestyle here and now.

A LOOK INTO THE FUTURE

A look into the future reveals great times of encounter with God's glory. With greater knowledge and understanding, and a more intimate relationship with our heavenly Father, we can enjoy a life based on John 4:24, when the worship experience of believers is total.

The language of the saints has changed into speaking to each other and to the Lord in psalms, hymns and spiritual songs, making melody in our hearts to the Lord.

There is a change in our corporate worship services because our attitudes have changed into that of constant expression of gratitude to God for His mercies.

Church is actually now a gathering to share in what the Lord is doing with and through us, rather than just desiring to be prayed for, day after day.

The glory of the Lord has filled the earth as the worship and the testimony of the saints is now abundant in the land.

These generations of Christians are blessed because the experience of the presence of the Lord is an everyday affair. Experiencing God's presence in worship has become a regular phenomenon.

The ministry of true worship has taken its proper place in the life of the individual believer and the entire church. The dwelling place of God with men is in a greater measure because God is left with only one obligation-to dwell in the praise and worship of His people, which comes up as a sweet-smelling savor to Him day after day.

The people living in this day are not at a loss concerning what to do with the abundance of knowledge and understanding of true worship. Nobody is asking them to worship the Lord because knowledge of the Lord and His worship has become the order of the day.

There is such a hush and mighty manifestation of the presence of His Majesty's glory in the corporate gathering of God's people and their individual and personal fellowship with the Lord.

There are so many mounting needs, yet the fire of the Lord's glory and presence consumes every sickness, disease, sorrow, curse and all infirmities. All live as if there is no need, just because of the revival of the worship of God.

The joy of the Lord has become the strength, health, prosperity, peace and longevity of these people because they, as His Majesty's subjects, now frequent the chambers where His awesome presence and tangible glory reside.

There are no words to describe this exciting experience!

Open our eyes Lord:

- That we may see You as we should

- That we may know You in entirety

- That our knowledge of You may be deepened

- That our experience of You will be enriched

- That our walk with You on earth will be richer

- That our spirits will be lost in Your greatness

- That the song of Your worship will continually be the very lives we live.

Lord, give us the true worship experience.

AUTHOR CONTACT

United States of America:
Rev. Eric Kwapong,
His Presence Ministries,
P. O. Box 4245,
Cary, N.C. 27519.
+ 919 460 9139

United Kingdom of Great Britian:
29 Croydon House,
Gloucester Road,
Tottenham, London N17 6LL
+ 44 208 352 9255

Ghana West Africa:
P.O. Box KN 779,
Kaneshie, Accra, Ghana.
+ 233 21 308284

Website: www.hpmin.org
Email: info@hpmin.org
          ekwapong@hpmin.org

SPECIAL SALUTE TO THESE GALLANT SERVANTS
OF GOD WHO ARE HUMBLY AND PASSION-
ATELY TOUCHING LIVES AND BRINGING THEM
TO THE KING OF GLORY:

BISHOP T.D. JAKES
DR. MYLES MUNROE
DR. KINGSLEY FLETCHER
DR. MENSA OTABIL
APOSTLE PAPA EZEKIEL GUTI
BISHOP NICHOLAS DUNCAN-WILLIAMS
BISHOP BOB HAWKSON
APOSTLE ANDREW WUTAWUNAHIE
REV. SAM LARBI
DR.GEORGE FERGUSON LAING
REV. MICHAEL ESSEL
BISHOP CHARLES AGYIN-ASARE
DR. SETH ANYOMI
REV. SAM KORANCHIE-ANKRAH
REV. EBENEZER MARKWEI
BISHOP NII NABI TACKIE-YARBOI
BISHOP DAG HEWARD-MILLS
REV. GHANDI OLAOYE
DR. ISAAC QUAYE
REV. ROBERT AMPIAH-KWOFIE
REV. STEVE MENSAH
REV. JUANITA MINCEY
BISHOP ROBERT WINLEY
REV. WILLIAM OBENG-DARKO
REV. KOFI GYAMERAH AKO
DR. SHADRACH OFOSUWARE

REV. CELIA APEAGYEI-COLLINS
REV. AGU IRUKWU
BISHOP DARLINGSTON JOHNSON
REV. CLEMENT ASIHENE
BISHOP LESLIE BUABASAH
REV. EMILY BUABASAH
REV. STANLEY MENSAH
DR. LAWRENCE TETTEH
DR. SOLA FOLA-ALADE

These men and women represent only a tiny fraction of many more gallant servants of God who for space, do not have their names here, but live and breathe the Father's Heart.